THE GREAT IMPOSTOR

The Great Impostor

ROBERT CRICHTON

Random House New York

NINTH PRINTING

© Copyright, 1959, by Robert Crichton
All rights reserved under International and Pan-American Copyright
Conventions. Published in New York by Random House, Inc., and
simultaneously in Toronto, Canada, by Random House of Canada,
Limited.
Library of Congress Catalog Card Number: 59-5716
Manufactured in the United States of America
by The Colonial Press Inc.

Contents

1 The Great Impostor Apprehended 3

2 Lawrence: The Start 12

3 When the Going Was Good 16

4 When the Going Was Bad 23

5 Over the Hill to the Poorhouse and Gone 29

6 The Young Monk 39

7 The Young Cleric 44

8 The Soldier 50

9 The Sailor 58

10 The Young Monk—Again 66

11 The Travels of the Green Trunk 72

12 Dean of the School of Philosophy 91

13 The End of the Trunk 101

14 The Short Life of Cecil Boyce Harmann 113

15 Surgeon Lieutenant Cyr of the Royal Canadian Navy 122

16 Catherine 130

17 Surgeon Cyr to the Combat Zone 137

18 Surgeon Cyr to the Operating Table 144

19 Surgeon Cyr to Glory 159

20 Surgeon Cyr to Disgrace 164

21 Demara in the Dumps 171

22 B. W. Jones, The Man From Mississippi 174

23 Ol' Cap'n Jones, Texas Guard 181

24 Ol' Cap'n Jones, Texas Warden   184

25 B. W. in Bedlam   189

26 B. W. on the Lam   196

27 Demara and the Law   203

28 A Summing Up   208

29 The Reason Why   215

1

THE GREAT IMPOSTOR
APPREHENDED

On the very cold morning of February 14, 1956, Detective Troopers Millard Nickerson and James Milligan of th Maine state police boarded a Coast Guard cutter in Rock land and headed out into Penobscot Bay. They were bound for North Haven Island, a clump of sand and rock and pine which sits out in the bay with its back against the Atlantic Ocean.

The sky was gray, dark with swells of snow clouds which pressed inland, and the strong wind, coming hard off the bay, coated the cutter with frozen brine. It was not, as Milligan pointed out, a promising day for a manhunt.

"What's the charge on the man?" the skipper of the cutter asked.

"Cheating," Milligan said. The skipper gave them a look of deep disappointment.

"I would have thought it was murder at least to bring you out on a day like this. The men will be upset."

"Well, to hell with the men," Nickerson said with quiet finality. "This is not your ordinary cheater."

On North Haven they were fortunate in finding the island's only taxi, and they wound their way up a narrow road out of the village, by snowed-over farms and past boarded-up, dead-looking summer places which were joined to patches of pine, green and dark, deep with snow.

"Got some good teachers up to school this year, I hear," Nickerson said. There was, even by Maine standards, a long pause before the answer.

"Got a good crop," the driver finally said. "Got Dana Smith, a good solid man. Then we got this Martin Godgart. Come on the island out of the blue and done a fine job with the boys."

"That's the big, heavy-set fellow who always wears the crew cut?"

"That's the one. Know him?"

"We know about him," Milligan said.

"That's more than we do out here, by God. Says he's from Brooklyn, New York, but to hear him talk he's from all over the world. Of course, *I* think he spins some stretchers but then that don't bother me none. He's a good one. Got all the kids on the island in the Sea Scouts, teaches at the Baptist Sunday School, and played Santa Claus to all the poor kids. We got plenty of those, you know."

"I suspect you have," Milligan said.

"But I'll tell you this," the driver persisted. "We never had nothin' like *him* out here before."

"I suspect you haven't," Nickerson added.

The school, a large, somber, shingled affair, was not an appetizing place in which to learn. The detectives were upset to find that Godgart wasn't there.

"Don't tell me he's decided to make a run for it," Milligan said. "It would be like him."

Both men eyed the stretches of snowy fields and pine around them and shivered at the prospects of having to track their quarry down. A determined man, although he couldn't escape, could hold out a long time in them before being taken. As they turned to go back to the taxi and plan what to do next, an old, mud-spattered Chevrolet swung around them and then seemed to spin into the school parking area. Before the car had actually come to a full stop, the door had been flung open, and a massive, powerful-looking man climbed from behind the wheel and, with his head bent against the wind, started up the slope toward them. His arms swung from side to side and this, combined with his bulk, gave him the appearance of a graceful bear.

When he saw the detectives, a look of surprised hurt crossed his face and he stopped exactly as suddenly as if he had been shot. For a moment he seemed to teeter where he stood, unsure of whether he was going to fall forward or tip backward, then he finally came on ahead.

"I have a feeling I can be of help to you two men," he said softly. "What took you so long to get here?"

"Let's do it this way first," Nickerson said, flourishing a paper, a warrant for Godgart's arrest, in his hand. "You are Martin Godgart?"

"In a manner of speaking, yes," the big man said.

"Your real name is Ferdinand Waldo Demara, Jr., is that right?"

"Sometimes it's hard to say what my name is."

"Let's do this thing right," Milligan said. "This *is* an arrest."

"All right, then. I was born under that name but I use Fred W. Demara now." Nickerson was checking against a small notebook.

"Alias Martin Godgart?" he asked. The man nodded yes.

"Alias Dr. Robert Linton French?" There was another nod of yes.

The detective studied the list for what seemed a long time.

"My," he said, "that Dr. French really got around. You went places with him."

"I did. He was one of my best," the teacher agreed.

"Alias Brother John Payne?"

"Alias Dr. Cecil Boyce Hamann?"

"You people have been doing your homework. Yes, I was him too."

"Alias Ben W. Jones, assistant warden of the Huntsville Prison in Texas?"

"I'm not ashamed of that one."

"Alias Dr. Joseph C. Cyr, surgeon lieutenant in the Royal Canadian Navy?"

"One of my very best," the prisoner said. He saw that Nickerson was closing his notebook. "Go ahead, go ahead. You've missed some."

"I think we've got enough to establish the case," Nickerson said with obvious irony.

"Enough to put you in jail for fifty years," Milligan said, not unnicely.

"If they *wanted* to put me in jail," the man, Demara, said. "Now if you don't mind, I'm beginning to freeze. I assume you want to take me in alive."

"Either way's all right," one of the detectives said, and they started back toward the schoolhouse. Demara didn't go with them but instead started back for his car.

"I don't want to go back in there. I'm clean in there and I want to keep it that way, please."

They started to follow him, but from a feeling of needlessly intruding they stopped and stayed where they were. They watched him rummaging through a pile of clothes and books in the back seat.

"If you're worried I have a gun down here, don't," he called. "I do, I mean, but I wouldn't shoot anyone and I wouldn't shoot myself. Know why? I'm afraid I'd miss myself and I couldn't stand that. I'd look ridiculous."

He put on a heavy gray greatcoat with a fur collar and then a black Navy watch cap.

"I'm going to look ridiculous back on the mainland in this outfit," Demara grumbled. "You know, of all the things I hate, I hate looking ridiculous the most."

The ride back to the harbor was stiffly silent. Occasionally the big man leaned forward and studied the landscape as if he were trying to burn it into his memory by sheer force. When they passed the American Legion hall he groaned at the sight of the shuttered windows.

"That's the town's social center. You know what day it is?" he asked. Besides the date no one did.

"This is Saint Valentine's Day. Do you see any sign of it here? Think someone might spend just one dollar on decorations, on little love tokens? To hell they would."

He stared morosely out the window, tapping the window with his nails. "These people broke away from the Massachusetts Puritans because they thought they were too frivolous, you know. They don't believe in loving their children because it's sort of sinful to show emotion." He smacked the fist of one hand into the palm of the other. "Oh, God, I had so much work to do here. Then you had to come out and get me," he ended bitterly.

At the dock, when they had piled out into the patches of wet snow, Demara suddenly let out a shattering whoop and began laughing, laughing so hard that he doubled over and began choking and puffing and the tears streamed down his face, steaming in the cold and turning the moonlike cheeks a glowing red.

"This takes the whole codfish cake," he finally managed. "Oh, God, this takes the cake," he shouted, pointing to the cutter tossing at the pier. "They've come for me in trains and planes, in cars and with the FBI. The cops have come. The MPs have tried. But, man, this is the first time they ever called out the fleet. I've never been more flattered."

When his tears and shaking stopped, he began picking up his things from the snow and heading toward the cutter.

"I don't know what they got on you, Martin," the taxi driver called, "but I want you to know that we stand behind you, Martin."

Demara didn't turn around until he was near the pier but then he called out to the man, who was already in his car, "Tell them to keep the Sea Scouts going, will you? It's all they got. And tell the Widow Crockett not to keep dinner hot. I'm not coming home."

They watched the car wind its way back up to the village.

"You know what you just heard?" Demara asked. "He called me 'Martin.' That means I belong now. I always find a home, I'm always just belonging when someone comes and takes me away and I'm a stranger again. I'm very tired of that now."

From a face dark and almost sunken with gloom, Demara suddenly smiled a bright, completely open smile. "Well, shall we away? My cutter waits."

The sun was attempting to break through and occasionally a flash touched some section of the water, causing it to sparkle and dance with sudden and startling animation. It occurred to Nickerson that that was the way it was with his prisoner.

On the wharf a door was banging and thumping against a shed wall every time a gust of wind blew in off the bay. As they passed it Demara put down an armload of his things and latched it shut. As he did so he caught the detectives eyeing each other with obvious approval of his act.

"Don't let that fool you," he said harshly. "You think I did that out of the goodness of my heart? If you do, there's one thing you should learn about me right now."

He didn't say what it was but picked up his things again, threaded along the ice-clear path on the pier and started down the ladder.

"All right. What is it?" Milligan finally asked.

"That I'm rotten," he answered sweetly. "Every bone in my body is rotten. I'm rotten through and through!"

On board the cutter the prisoner was treated with the respect Americans generally reserve for captured criminals. The voices of the seamen were hushed as one after another they found an excuse to file through the wardroom and examine him. He very quickly amazed them with his knowledge of the ship and the questions he asked.

When he saw Nickerson eyeing him quizzically, he shouted at him, "Why do you look at me like that? You know my credentials. You know my past. I could take this cutter across the Atlantic and bring it right back to this spot again."

When they were several miles out to sea he asked permission to go on deck and take a last look at the island. The wind was whipping up a fine spume and it wet their faces. Not all the wetness was from the sea. Nickerson was surprised to see that his prisoner was crying. The sun was out over North Haven, and against the hard iron of the water the island's snow glowed with a whiteness that seemed to be lit from within.

"Do you know a play called 'The Playboy of the Western World'?"

One of the two said that he did.

"There's one of the saddest lines in all the world in there," Demara said. "It's near the end and Pegeen Mike has lost her man. He wasn't much but he was all she had and she'd learned to love him. That's the way I feel about North Haven."

The snow had already begun to merge into the hemlock greenness of the pines and soon they became a part of each other. Soon the island had merged with the rocks of the shore and then that merged with the sea until that strange moment when everyone realized there was nothing.

"Like the line from the play," he continued sadly. "I've lost my only Haven in the western world."

They turned to go back down and as they did so, the cutter took a sharp turn south toward Rockland, taking the swells on her starboard side. The ship began to roll and the men grabbed suddenly for the railings.

"Wouldn't that be ridiculous if I went overboard? I can see the headlines now. Full Fathom Five The Fat Fake Lies. Ridiculous!"

They began warily making their way down the deck to the wardroom.

"If I had any self-respect I would go right over the side," he said glumly.

"You wouldn't do that," Nickerson said. "You love life too much."

"I don't love life," Demara said easily. "I hate life. It disgusts me."

"You know you're trouble," Nickerson insisted. "I've studied that record of yours too much not to know. You expect too much out of life and when it doesn't pan out you break and run or you put on a disguise."

The statement appeared to enrage the man for at least the moment.

"This is so typical of my luck. Everyone else gets arrested by a cop. I got to get arrested by a disciple of Freud," he said.

"No. One last point," Nickerson persisted. "Every time you take on a new identity the whole world opens up for you, doesn't it? I mean, it's all fresh and wide open like the day you left home."

"Now I'm telling you the truth and then I don't want any more of this bull. Every time I take a new identity," Demara said steadily, "some part of the real me dies, whatever the real me is."

He went over to a couch and sprawled out on it. "Now, if the analytical session is over I think I'll take a nap." He pulled his greatcoat over him and in a minute, with that abandon and innocence of childhood, he appeared to be fast asleep.

"In all my years," Milligan said, "this is the damnedest arrest I've been on. How do you account for the guy?"

From across the room, muffled by the coat, came Demara's voice.

"We impostors, sir, are unaccountable people." After that came the sound of snoring.

"You've got to remember one thing," Milligan explained. "This guy didn't just assume the name or the titles like most impostors. He lives the lives and does the jobs."

"As I said once before," Nickerson said, "this is not your *ordinary* cheater."

Detective Trooper Nickerson had said true.

Fred W. Demara was tried in Augusta for "cheating by false premises," found guilty and, as happens with almost every institution he has defrauded, in order to save themselves embarrassment, they didn't choose to press charges. While in prison a delegation of people came over to the mainland to plead in his defense and ask him to return to North Haven with all forgiven and a fresh start promised. He refused. "I wouldn't want my children to be taught by a known impostor. It's all right if they don't know, of course."

Demara was put on probation in the State of Maine, and then set free when he let it be known that he planned to leave the state.

As almost always, Demara went home again.

2

Home is Lawrence, Massachusetts, where he was born Ferdinand Waldo Demara, Jr., on December 12, 1921. A newspaper of the day describes it as being cold and cloudy, a cheerless winter day in New England—one of the few simple facts about an otherwise wildly cluttered life.

The birth was a highly festive occasion. Ever since the birth of his first child, Elaine, Demara, Sr., had been hungry for an heir. For several days the greats of Lawrence, what there was of them, streamed through the big Victorian house on Jackson Street, then the finest street in town, and clucked with admiration at the boy. None of them was conscious of the forces already at work on the big baby in the lavish bassinet, but they were real and they were enough to cause a split in his personality that never was to heal.

The boy's father was of French-Canadian stock and had arrived in Lawrence by way of Providence, Rhode Island, in the hopes of getting rich. He very nearly did. There was about him an exotic quality alien to New England, as surprising as the flash of a scarlet tanager in a corn field. No matter how far he was removed from them there was always the faint far echo of the boulevards of Paris in his bearing, and all of his life possessed that most un-Yankee-like trait: an irresistible flair for the flamboyant.

The baby's mother, Mary McNelly of Massachusetts-Irish origin, was another kettle of fish entirely. She was the product of a careful Catholic upbringing in which religious dogma is inseparably married to lace-curtain gentility, and decorum is next to godliness. The end result is an advanced interest in duty, discipline and a repression of man's baser instincts. To compound this, her rearing took place in the singular city of Salem, that witch's brew of unreconstructed Puritanism which has never been able to resolve its dilemma that in all the years it was trying to save its collected soul it earned its collective living by trafficking in luxuries from the pagan Orient. The gateway to the corruptions of Cathay were only as far away as the stern harbor mouth of Salem.

And there was always the memory of Salem's ancestors, those who had been burned and stoned for witches and those who had done the burning and the piling on of stones. To develop a flowering sense of guilt and sin, Salem has choice soil.

It was not the fashion of the time for Irish girls to marry French-Canadians—Canucks they were called and looked on as something unreliable—but Mary McNelly did and for many years had no reason to regret it. The early days in Lawrence were happy days.

As strange a city as Salem is by American standards, in its fashion Lawrence is even stranger. Lying in a shallow valley between the ancient towns of Methuen and Andover on the banks of the fast-flowing Merrimack, the city was created by a holding company before the Civil War to do just one thing: produce textiles. Acres of sensible red bricks, some of the world's largest mills and hard by them, the world's biggest workers' dormitories, carpeted the valley floor. From the start housing was inadequate. When the mills expanded and housing didn't, Lawrence was, while still in its infancy, on its way to civic senility and to becoming a colossal industrial slum.

The original workers were Yankee farm girls from overcrowded New England farms, but when they no longer would go to Lawrence because of bad conditions, the mill

owners, in collusion with steamship operators, began recruiting from among the most deprived people of Europe
and the Mediterranean area—the people, they figured, who
would be most likely to find Lawrence bearable.

> *Give me your tired, your poor,*
> *Your huddled masses yearning to be free* . . .

Emma Lazarus' words cried out on the base of the Statue
of Liberty, and the mill operators heard them. From the
slums of Athens and Naples, the farms of Sicily, from Tur-
key and Armenia, and the bazaars of Syria and Damascus
the owners brought them, and after them came people from
Central Europe and the Balkans and the Baltic coast.

Every belief, from Mohammedan to Jewish to Coptic and
Catholic, from Syrian Orthodox, Russian Orthodox and un-
orthodox was soon represented. There were freethinkers,
foul thinkers, and pagans; the tough and the breakable, the
wise and bewildered, the corrupt and those who had somehow retained something of the divine. They were, in short,
the sum of humanity and they were all thrown together into
the Lawrence melting pot. The trouble was that they didn't
melt. In Lawrence there was no America to melt into. The
result was a series of enclaves—islands of each nationality
clinging together like barnacles on pier piles—clustering
with each other in rows of crowded, rotting buildings.

"Wherever I went in Lawrence, except on Jackson Street,
I was always a stranger," Demara has said.

The renowned Lawrence strike, one of the most bitter in
American labor history, while it momentarily united many
of the diverse groups in Lawrence, also helped to split the
city into two hostile, warring factions which never have
made peace. The old labor password of "Which side are
you on, brother?" has rarely had more meaning.

This was the world that the baby was inheriting. A city
of nearly 100,000 people from fifty lands who spoke seventy

languages and dialects. And a city so hopelessly tied to one industry that it never even remotely knew the rhythm of American life. When the mills were open the people lived and when they shut the people died—all of them. It was then either boom or bust. You either were a cynic or a hopeless optimist; that was the only way to survive it. You never planned ahead. You took the chance and trusted to your personal fate and luck.

It can't be said that Lawrence produces impostors but it can be argued that if a person has some bent toward impostoring and the roots for it are there, they couldn't find a better place for them to seize hold and flourish. Such prosaic restraints on a boy's lively imagination as tradition and stability were almost totally lacking in Lawrence. The situation was fluid and there were people who drowned in it every day in Lawrence.

3

WHEN THE GOING WAS GOOD

Of all the days of Fred Demara's early life one stands alone in its vividness. It was his fourth birthday and there had been a party. The children were going, slipping down icy steps and leaving trails across the snowy lawn, and he was calling out "Thank you for coming to my party" as his mother had told him to do. When he went back into the house the paper plates and hats were gone, but his father and mother were standing at the foot of the big curving staircase, and the big cutglass chandelier, which was only lit for very special times, was glowing. The closing of the door caused the glass to shimmer, and sparks of light flashed on the deep-red rug and ran glittering along the walls.

He knew something nice was going to happen. Next to his parents but a little behind them stood the house staff, smiling and attentive. Beneath the direct light of the chandelier he felt aflame, bathed in the liquid purity coming down like the pictures of the saints he saw in church. Only his sister Elaine, staring moodily down at him through the railings on the banister, seemed wrong.

"Today my son is four years old," his father said, "and on this day he becomes a little man."

His father looked so elegant in his morning coat with his fresh blue boutonniere. "From this day on I shall expect all of you to address the young master with the respect due to him. Beginning tonight he is to be called Mr. Demara. I will expect it of you and so shall he."

There was a light spatter of applause and each servant took a step forward in turn, made the very faintest sort of bow, and said, "Happy birthday, *Mr.* Demara."

As they did so, the boy, with a sudden instinct for the proper thing and the dramatic moment, went to a table on which a vase of roses stood and took four of them. To each of the servants he gave a rose. It became a legend in the family.

The only sour note came from the stairs. "Mr. Demara," Elaine sneered and ran to her room, where Fred later found her crying.

Their money came from movies. While a projectionist in Providence, Demara, Sr., had saved his money and used Sunday as a day for scouring New England for a spot to open his own theater. At the sight of Lawrence, as dismal as it was, Demara's heart leaped with joy. The sight of the streets filled with lounging and leaning people inspired him. Here was a town starved for entertainment. No one else had tried movies here because it was reasoned that you couldn't very well show a film with thirty different sub-titles, but Demara was showman enough to realize that a pie tossed in the face of a man wearing a high hat or a po-liceman's badge meant a laugh in any language.

With the help of a man named Toomey, who supplied some cash and much local influence, a store was leased, chairs were rented and, running a steady diet of slapstick comedies, the Toomey-Demara Amusement Company was born. It was a howling success. Mobs of mill hands poured in and out of the store like a Cecil B. DeMille riot scene at its wildest. In very short time Toomey-Demara had enough money to build The Palace—a glorious monument to the cinema arts and to Lawrence, one of the wonders of the world. In quick fashion, to keep out outside competition, T-D built The Broadway, The Modern and The Empire, which showed the way the two men were thinking.

After that the Demaras moved from a boarding house near the mills to Jackson Street. By Lawrence standards they had arrived.

Although they were rich and were Catholic, Fred was entered in the local public school, which was called the Emily G. Weatherbee School. His parents didn't want any child of theirs getting spoiled or pampered treatment and the Catholic school was too far away.

From his first year he felt different and out of place. His family was the only one he knew that didn't work directly for the mills. Many of the children in school were very poor and his clothes never looked like the others' clothes. And he looked different. Pictures of him then show a curious richness and elaborateness about them which was strange to his mother and alien to Lawrence. His father rather liked it.

He was larger than any of the children his age and his hair was long, dark and possessed a luxurious sheen. His eyebrows were dark and long as were his lashes, and his eyes, which by all rights should have been brown, were a startling, striking blue.

He was a lonely boy because the others left him alone, but he doesn't remember minding that. He was the kind of boy who could entertain himself for endless hours at a time. When he did play with other children, he had two rules. He didn't like games of physical violence and when he played he wanted to be leader or he didn't want to play. He had two things that worked in his favor. He was immensely strong and he had, oddly enough, an unexplained, wild rage. In a rage he would hold his breath until he turned almost dark purple and he was capable of smashing things. He frightened the others in school and they let him alone.

In the fifth grade, however, they didn't, and he had a first brush with the law. A boy who was punished for doing something wrong became convinced that Fred had ratted on him. In indignation a vigilante mob was formed to mete out justice for the worst sin known to all childhood—telling on someone to a grown-up.

"We're going to get you at lunch. All of us. We're going to gouge out your eyes and smash your face," he was told.

At mid-morning recess he went home and when he came back his face wore a bland, unworried look that only provoked the others all the more. At noon they got him near some monkey bars and began prodding him toward the bars until his back touched them and he could go no farther. When the next boy touched him he reached up under his jacket and beneath his sweater and pulled out a large and terrifying dueling pistol.

"I'm going to shoot your guts out," he screamed and advanced on the boys. Every one of them found some different way to get out of the Emily G. Weatherbee schoolyard. A little later that afternoon the police came to school and from Fred's school bag they took two pistols, and then they took Fred away.

It made him, of course, a hero and for a week at least he was the object of undisguised worship.

"I remember it felt good to be one of the guys. I had never felt like I belonged anywhere."

The only way he knew of belonging was to do something bad. From one of the best-behaved boys in the school he quickly became one of the worst. It got so bad, finally, that it was suggested to his family that he be taken out and put in another school.

"Maybe that was the beginning of the pattern. Just when I belonged, I didn't," Demara says. They took him out of Weatherbee School and entered him in St. Augustine's, a Roman Catholic parochial school.

For the first time in his life he had a serious dispute with his family. He made up his mind that he wasn't going to speak either at school or at home until he was returned to his old school. For weeks he held out against all the pressures that were exerted against him until one afternoon, sitting sullenly in study hall, he heard the soft sound of shoe leather come up behind him and felt the presence of someone hovering over him. It was the mother superior of the school and she simply sat down beside him and draped her black knit cloak around him as if he were being enveloped by the wing of some warm, kindly bird.

At first he resisted her but there was something far more powerful than his stubborn boy's will. In the secrecy of the cloak he began sobbing and crying helplessly about some sorrow he couldn't name. He can still recapture the feeling of being reborn into the world again as he cried.

Sitting beside her, he became gradually terribly conscious of the crucifix she wore until, he feels, that he was perhaps hypnotized by it.

"I don't know, but I decided right then I had some special sacred mission and I made up my mind to become a very devout boy."

He did what he had promised himself. He became almost at once the most loyal, hardest-working altar boy in St. Augustine's.

"It was very strange to me even then. I became very happy and very calm. There were some sad days, I guess, but now I can only see them as happy days. It never rained or was cold in my memory of those days. Everything was always all green and gold. The grass in front of the house was fresh and green and the sun coming through the trees was rich and golden when I was very young."

The rich, warm, all-embracing sweet solemnity of the Church and its rituals was a cloak which shielded him from outside shocks. He began spending a great deal of his time in the sacristy. The pictures of him at the time show him to possess a fine, white, beatific quality, delicate for all his great size, and his enormous eyes, far-looking blue circles of innocence, especially when seen against the black cloth of an acolyte's habit, were an impressive sight.

He loved to mouth the words of the Church. The names of the priestly vestments were recited like a litany.

> *Amice, Alb and Cincture,*
> *Maniple, Chasuble and Stole,*
> *Surplice, Cope, Humeral Veil,*
> *Cassock, Dalmatic and Tunic.*

And then there were the special insignia belonging to the office of bishop. The exotic richness of the words was enough to grip the imagination of any impressionable boy

> *Pectoral Cross and Gremial Veil,*
> *Miter, Gloves and Ring,*
> *Buskins and Sandals,*
> *Cappa Magna and Tunicles,*
> *Zuchetto, Morse and Mantelletta.*

When he wanted something very bad or when he felt he was in trouble he recited the words as his own private prayer. He also had a dream that someday he would be wearing a bishop's insignia although he never mentioned it to anyone.

How the dream was to wither! Years later, in a dispute over title to a car, in a stroke of giant irony, Demara threatened to turn the matter over to his lawyers, the distinguished firm of Zuchetto, Morse and Mantelletta.

And he is still fond of telling people who ask him where he gets the dark, clerical-looking suits he prefers that they come from the firm of Cassock, Dalmatic and Tunic. No one has yet blinked an eye.

But then, when the going was all gold and green and he was gently laved in the love of the faith, there was no hint of such things to come. Although it seemed odd to many of the people in St. Augustine's, everyone had to admit that of all the boys in the school, the Demara boy was the one who most seemed to have a genuine vocation for the priesthood and who showed the greatest promise of them all for the future.

4

He was coming across the lawn late one afternoon early in autumn, making a trail in the yellow leaves, when he saw Elaine leaning against a pillar on the porch. It was one of those soft, smoky days. Down the street someone was burning leaves and there was a haze and the slanting sun coming through it in shafts here and there left glittering pools of gold. Elaine was standing in one and he recalls how delicate her beauty looked but also how strangely she looked at him wading across the grass. He remembers it all because it was a day he was never to forget.

"Mama and Papa are waiting for you," she said. There was something about the tone of her voice which caused him to feel frightened.

"Is anything wrong?" he asked, although he didn't want to hear it from her.

"It's something real bad," Elaine said.

Inside the house it was still and silent and Mrs. Larch, the housekeeper, had forgotten to turn on the lights. He stood before the mirror looking at himself to find the courage to go upstairs when he heard his father's low voice talking swiftly and then he thought he heard his mother crying. He stood, undecided what to do—he didn't want to see his mother crying—when he realized his father was at the head of the stairs looking down on him.

"Come upstairs now, son," he said softly, almost apologetically, as if he was the one who had done wrong. In his parents' dressing room his mother sat next to the window, like Elaine downstairs, bathed in the sun's last rays. Looking into the light, he could not see her face, but a handkerchief in her hand let him know she had been crying and when she turned to him he saw the redness of her eyes.

"How can I tell you this?" his father said.

"Just tell him the truth," his mother said. "He's a big boy now. He's eleven years old and can stand to hear the truth when his father tells it."

He knew what it was. One of them had cancer and was going to die.

"Now try and follow this," his father said in a weak voice. It wasn't like him at all. "All of these things? All of this around us?"

"Yes, Father?"

"You're going to be brave about this, aren't you, son?" Why did he ask? He was going to be brave but he felt himself weakening. Why wouldn't his father just say what it was?

"None of this belongs to us any more. Someone is going to come and take it away," he said.

"We're going to have to move away, son," his mother said. "You see, Daddy has lost all his money."

"But why do we have to move away?" he suddenly blurted out. "This is our home. You don't need money to live in your home because it's your home." He knew he was lying to himself but he wanted to say it and hoped someone would say that he was right.

"Oh, we'll get some more money, all right, son," his father said, and ran his hand through Fred's soft brown hair.

"And then we'll come back," Fred said.

"We'll certainly try, Fred. We'll try," his father said forcibly.

"Fred," his mother's voice came across the room cold and hard.

"Don't tell the boy lies. He's old enough to know. He's got to know."

"But I'm telling the truth. I'm going to try and we're going to be all right again, I promise you." He turned to the boy. "Now, you're going to be brave about this," he said. "I know you are. Say that you're going to be a brave little soldier."

"I'll be brave, Daddy," he answered, and he hoped he would be. "Can I go down, now?"

Downstairs he felt he had to get out of the dark, musty house into the fresh air. Elaine was still leaning against the pillar but the sun had moved away and she was in shadows.

"Well, did he tell you?" she asked. "What did he say?"

"Oh, nothing," Fred said.

"Oh, yes, he did," Elaine said. "We've lost all our money and we're going to move. That's what."

"That's nothing," he said easily. "He's going to get it back again and then we're going to move back."

"Oh, no, we're not, we're not coming back. Ever."

"Who said?"

"Mother said, that's who said. We're *poor!*"

"That's not what Papa said. We're coming back. It's just like a vacation."

"Oh, no, we're not!"

"We are."

"This is silly. I'm cold. I'm going in now. We have to pack. Mama says we have to move Saturday." She danced across the porch to the front door. "I'm going to miss this porch."

"We are coming back though, aren't we?" he said.

"We're *not*. Not, not, not." She opened the door and said sadly, "We're poor people now. We don't belong here any more."

He stayed out on the lawn until the street lights flickered on and the shadows were eerily long and he was cold. The house was very dark. He went in the back way because he didn't want to face his family, but in the kitchen he found his mother cooking supper by the light of several candles.

"Where's Cook?" he asked.

"We had to ask the cook to leave, Fred."

"Oh," he said. "Where are the lights?"

"They turned them off."

"Oh." So that was what being poor was like.

In the dining room, since there was no one to serve dinner, they all huddled at one end of the large table under candlelight.

"Just like the pioneers used to do," his mother said cheerfully. "There'll be all kinds of new adventures."

No one said anything. The food was from cans and was not very hot, and every time Fred thought of Mrs. Larch and the cook and Maria, the last serving girl, his stomach felt funny and he lost his appetite. Most of all, the sight of his father staring at his food, seeming to try to lose himself in the shadows outside the light of the candles, scared him.

"Aw, this is no fun," he said. He felt if he stayed there any longer he would begin to cry or shiver with fright. He dropped his spoon and ran for the darkness of the stairwell.

"Son!" He heard his father call. "Now, sonny, you come back here. You promised to be brave."

"This is no fun at *all*," he called down.

In his room he felt safe again, as if what he had seen downstairs was some kind of charade. On his bureau he had a little shrine dedicated to the Blessed Virgin Mary in front of which there were flowers he had picked and little cards, pretty things he found, and two votive lights, which he lit. The familiar blue flickering light reassured him.

There was his bed, all nicely turned down, and under his pillow were his pajamas. He slid his toes along through the soft, warm rug and he climbed into his soft, warm bed. He knew that if he prayed hard enough and hoped hard enough everything was going to be all right.

"Please, Little Jesus and Mother Mary," he whispered,

"please don't make us poor. If you don't I'll say a rosary every night of my life." With the bargain being struck he went softly, warmly to sleep.

On Saturday morning it was raining, but the moving van came and a man from the bank to tell them what they could take and what they must leave. He sat in the front seat of their big touring Pierce Arrow, watching the rain wash down the celluloid windows, refusing to move. Once his sister handed him a sandwich, which he didn't eat, and another time his mother came to warn him that whatever he failed to take from his room would be left behind. He took nothing. They would be back. Much later, when it was nearly dark, everyone came and climbed wetly into the car.

"Good-bye, old house," Elaine called as the car started up. "We loved you, old house." She looked at her brother. "Aren't you going to say good-bye?"

"Why should I?" he said. "We'll be back soon."

They followed the great clumsy van, and in the wet gloom it looked like a whale wallowing in surf. They wound down into town, past the hulks of the silent, empty mills, around through the rows of dormitories and then back out and up Andover Street.

"We'll be back, won't we, Dad?" The boy kept nodding wisely to himself. "We'll be back."

The rain had caused a flood of leaves to slither off the trees, and Fred could actually hear the rubber of the tires hissing through them as they turned. He has never since been able to attend a funeral without thinking of that day or hearing that sound of wet rubber hissing.

The house, on the outskirts of Lawrence, was an old carriage house with servants' quarters, part of a once grand estate. The head mover was waiting for them impatiently. On Jackson Street, Fred had noticed how careful the movers were to cover the furniture and see that no scratches occurred.

"What'll we do with this stuff?" the foreman asked. "We'll never get it in *there*."

His attitude and voice were disrespectful and unpleasant. Fred saw his father begin to angrily open his mouth to say something but then quietly close it again.

"Well, I suspect we'll just have to store some of it in that barn down there, won't we?" he said meekly.

That was not like his father at all.

Fred found he had to share a room with Elaine, and very early, after a cold dinner, they went to bed to get warm. The cots were separated from each other by a drape which pulled across a wire. The cots were hard and there were no sheets and the blankets were stiff and scratchy.

"I miss my bed, don't you?" he asked into the darkness.

"Uh-huh," Elaine answered. "Go to sleep now."

"I really hate it here, don't you? I want to go back."

"No," his sister said. "Mother said you weren't being brave."

That hurt him. He knew it was true.

"Did she *really* say that?"

"Uh-hmm. When she was crying. Can't you *try* to like it here?"

He could try. He would try, at least until they got ready to go back.

"All right, I'll try. But it isn't going to be easy."

5

OVER THE HILL

TO THE POORHOUSE AND GONE

It wasn't easy. The male Demaras did not know how to be poor. Being poor is either an inherited condition or else an art and an instinct and in both of these the Demaras were deprived.

Young Fred hated the feel of corduroy against his legs and he hated the whirring noise the material made when his pants legs rubbed against each other. Even worse was the feel of blue jeans, the ugliness of the color when they were new but, worst of all, their stink, thick with the smell of poverty and defeat. He rebelled and stayed away three days from school when his mother brought a pair of shoes home from the repairman, and caps, not quite the same color as the rest of his shoes, were sewn across the front of the toes so he couldn't scuff through. After that she bought him a pair of "sensible" black work boots, heavy and stiff, "just like the mill hands wore." They humiliated him and he found a way of beating them. With the few pennies he somehow managed to earn and save he bought a pair of shoes and hid them in a wooden box at the end of the walk leading out to the Andover Road. No matter what the weather, he always changed, out of sight of his mother, into his own shoes and hid the black ones in the box.

Instead of bringing him closer to the other boys in school, most of whom were poor boys, his family's poverty only separated him more. As a poor boy he was poor in a wrong way and the others knew it and resented it. Furthermore

the longer he stayed away from Jackson Street, the more
he turned away from the Church. His prayers were going
unanswered, his pact with Little Jesus was not being honored, and he was fast losing all interest and, finally, all faith.
The flame of religious passion, which only months before
consumed much of his life, was a cold ash.

It was in his last year at St. Augustine's that Demara became involved in an incident that was to make life in Lawrence unbearable.

There was on St. Valentine's day an annual ritual where
the older boys symbolically turned over their class to the
class coming along. Each eighth grader sponsored a seventh
grader. Part of the ceremony was an exchange of simple
little gifts. On an impulse Fred decided that he would show
them all how a boy born on Jackson Street behaved. The
evening before the party he went to a bakery-candy shop
off Jackson Street, where his family still had a charge account although it was almost never used, and he ordered a
large, two-pound, heart-shaped, glowing red box of chocolates to be delivered at *exactly* three o'clock the next afternoon to Sister Veronica's room at St. Augustine's. It was so
promised.

At a quarter to three the next day he was beginning to be
tense. He was the only boy in the room without a present.
He was not really worried because they had promised him
and he believed them. But at three o'clock he was covered
with sweat and he could hear his heart pounding. Also at
three o'clock Sister Veronica began calling out sponsor's
names.

"Francy Connors, sponsor of Tony Strubik." Francy
walked across the classroom, shook Tony's hand, gave him
his present and then led him back across the room. When
Demara's name was called he found he couldn't force himself to move.

"Cross over to Vincent. You needn't be ashamed if you
have no present," Sister Veronica whispered.

"I *have* a present. I bought one. The most expensive present they ever had here," he said.

"Now there's no reason to fib," the nun said sharply. "We don't have to lie about it."

The boys around him were snickering and he could feel his face reddening.

"I'm not lying. The man was supposed to deliver it. He promised. He promised, Sister. At three o'clock." He looked at the clock, which read ten past three, and the class roared with laughter.

"He's in the hall now maybe," Demara said. He ran to the door, for one brief moment sure he would find the candy man in the hall, but it was empty and when he turned back into the room tears began to swim into his eyes. They were laughing at him.

"You're the liars," he cried out. "Not me. You're the liars."

He could make out the shape of Sister Veronica coming toward him.

"You too. You too, Sister. You're like all the rest."

He ran to the door and out into the hall, slamming the door behind him with a crash that thundered hollowly down the hall. He ran to the heavy main doors, which were rarely opened, and pushed hard on them. Slowly the doors moved and then they flung open, sending him flying out into the brightness of the day, blinded but running hard, conscious of the jeers and cries from the lines of boys along the window above him, tasting the salt of his tears.

He walked and ran until he got to the hills of Methuen, where he had his own private secret place off the road. He built a small fire and soon he felt better. He felt snug and warm, safe from the wind and from being seen, warm in a cocoon of the fire's glow and his self-confidence was restored.

"The bastards," he said. "The little snot-nosed bastards."

That made him feel better. The moon was up, a new moon, a sickle of frost hooked in the sky, and that also made him feel better. Ever since he was very young he has felt he had an especial affinity with the moon. A new moon was a good sign. He stayed until that utterly royal blue of a clear, cold late-winter afternoon almost mysteriously slipped into blackness. Near him was a large dead cedar tree and he suddenly realized that the occasion, to be perfect, demanded a ritual of purification.

He took part of his little fire and carried it across to the base of the tree and then he began running. Down he went, running toward the lights in the valley that now beckoned to him, until behind him he sensed the whole hillside blossoming into flame. He turned to see a whoomph of yellow splash out into the blackness. He felt cleansed. He also had a plan.

The next day the others were amazed to see him in school. At three o'clock they were even more amazed. There was a scraping noise outside Sister Veronica's room and a head appeared in the room.

"Excuse me, Sister. You got a Mister Demara here?"

Before she could answer, Fred was going toward the door.

"I am Mister Demara," he said grandly. "Bring them in."

When the man came back in he was pushing a laundry hamper filled with satiny, heart-shaped boxes of chocolates.

"Where's the big one?" Fred asked. The deliveryman pulled a very large box from the hamper that drew an unintentional gasp of admiration from the class. "One for each," Mister Demara commanded.

They saw him go out into the hall and across it into the seventh-grade room where he delivered the big box to the Vincent boy he had left empty-handed the day before. Then they heard his heels go down the hall and felt a rush of cold air as the main doors opened, and closed with a ringing clang.

The children ran their fingers over the slick, tight cellophane, afraid to open the luxurious packages.

"Well, we might as well open them," Sister Veronica said grimly.

That night another tree burned on Methuen's hills. To the boy it was a glorious victory.

It was never the same in Lawrence after that. Almost no one spoke to him, and when they did they called him the Candy Butcher. The name and the incident continued to follow him when he moved on to Lawrence Central Catholic. He had a brief moment of glory when he went out for the varsity football team and actually made the squad, the only freshman ever to do it, but that didn't last long. He didn't like the discipline and he didn't like to hit people and he wouldn't learn the plays. He wasn't dropped. He just gradually ceased to belong to the team.

"I spent my days dreaming," he recalls now. "I walked around in the afternoons and even in the night and just dreamed about things I hoped would come true. I still felt that we were going to move back to Jackson Street and I used to go to the old house and sit in the attic of my old home and dream about things. Nothing could hurt me then and nothing could move me, either."

But that winter something happened that was to change the course of his life. His father, who was deeply worried about his son's loss of religion, finally persuaded the boy, under strong protest, to spend a week end with a cousin of the family, a Father Desmarais (the Demara branch had Anglicized the spelling), pastor of a parish in the heavily French-Canadian town of Woonsocket, Rhode Island, in the hope that Fred might be able to find God again.

In sullen anger, on a bitterly cold night in March, 1936, the boy stepped off a train at Woonsocket and, before he could get his bearings, found himself being relieved of his father's black Gladstone and ushered into a large, elegant black car. The door was shut behind him with a rich, metallic click, and with no words being spoken he was being driven swiftly through the town's grimy streets until they stopped in front of an old, elaborate house.

"This way, Master Demara," the driver said, and Fred was directed in through the front door and left waiting in the foyer. Overhead a lighted chandelier gently revolved and he could see into a paneled room softly and richly lit by subdued yellow lights. For the first time in so many years he was home again. He was back on Jackson Street, where he felt he belonged and was wanted.

He took an immediate and mutually shared liking for Father Desmarais, a tolerant, gentle but firm man, and he very quickly found himself pouring out his soul to this man he barely knew but hugely trusted. They talked about God, and in front of Father Desmarais it suddenly seemed ridiculous not to believe in God. His presence seemed all around Demara.

In his room that night his bed was turned down, but what he liked most was the feeling of the rug, soft and warm, sliding under his toes as he slipped across it. He opened the window and it was very cold but he scrunched down between the crisp, fresh sheets and under the comforter and he was warm and safe. He slept until noon of the next day. This was the way he was intended to live.

The next afternoon they went for a drive and along the way they passed a monastery of Trappist monks, a branch of the Cistercians, called Our Lady of the Valley. From inside the walls of the abbey they could hear the sound of men singing and in the fields outside they saw groups of quiet, cheerful, devout-looking men. Demara was struck by their silent comradeship.

"Of all the places in the world, this is where I would most like to be," Father Desmarais said. Coming from him this was high recommendation. The boy made a note not to forget it.

Several weeks after his return home, his sister Elaine died.

She had been shopping and had slipped on a patch of ice. When she came home she complained of a headache that aspirin wouldn't cure but she went ahead making dinner. After a little while she lay down to take a nap and she never got up. A depression settled over the house that wasn't lifted for months and the boy could hardly stand it. That despondency lasted until a day in the following spring when the telephone rang. The phone was one of the last luxuries they owned, not because it was a luxury but because it was Demara, Sr.'s last link with an outside world he dreamed someday would call again.

"It's for you, Fred," he heard his mother say. Her voice was trembling with excitement. "It's from *them*. The men downtown. The ones who bought the theaters."

His father leaped to his feet but then he sank back into his chair.

"Tell them I'm not here. Tell them I'm on a business appointment but will be back in an hour and will call then," he said.

"Oh Fred. No. You can't."

"Do it," he ordered, in a voice the boy hadn't heard in many years.

An hour later, in a voice as cool and deep as a radio announcer's, his father phoned that yes, he could just squeeze in a meeting downtown the next day.

That night there was joy in the house. "I knew they'd call. They *had* to call. They couldn't run it without the man who knows how to make them run. Now, get a steak. A big one. And I'll get the wine."

After dinner the men lolled majestically in their chairs while Mrs. Demara went to work restoring to their former glory the last of Mr. Demara's fine suits and shirts. Fred shined his father's shoes until they glowed, and warmed by the wine his father talked about the good times they had known and the good times that were ahead.

"Even if it's only managing *one* of the theaters, it's a way back. I'll make such a success of that they'll have to give me the others."

The boy waited, smelling the good cigar smell of his childhood, until the right moment. "Did you know that our old house on Jackson Street is still empty, Dad?" he asked.

"Nooo. You don't say, son?" his father said. He could see the far away look in his father's eyes and he knew what it meant, because it was in his eyes also.

At noon of the next day his father was dressed and ready to go and he was a splendid sight. He was, as his mother once told him, one of the few men in Lawrence who could carry a cane and sport spats and not look foolish doing it. At the end of the walk, from the old untended garden there, Mr. Demara retrieved a small flower and stuck it in his buttonhole. The boy yearned to run down to the edge of the street and wave his father off but he knew that wouldn't do. When the trolley came over the rise leading down to town and his father dropped his jitney in the coin box it looked for all the world as if he were doing the transit system a favor.

It was nearly dark when he came back. His flower was gone and the suit had an old, wilted look. He went into the house and into the darkness of the living room.

"Don't turn on the lights," he ordered and Fred knew then that he didn't want to see his father's face. "They offered me a *job*," his father finally said.

"That was good of them, wasn't it?" He heard his mother ask.

"A job," his father persisted, mercilessly. "The job of projectionist."

"Oh," his mother said. "You didn't take it?"

"Six bloody days a week. From noon until eleven at night." The boy wanted to leave, because he felt the voice was cracking and he was afraid of tears, of seeing his father cry.

"They want to pay me twenty-eight dollars a week."

"You didn't take it?" his mother asked.

"Of course, I took it," his father cried, and it was as if someone was actually then hurting him. "Of course, I took it. What else could I do? I'm a failure but not a bum, in the name of God." And he began crying.

Fred slipped out through the kitchen into the cold cleanliness of outside and for a moment pretended that he hadn't really heard all of what he had heard. But from the side window he could still hear his father, in anguish saying, "You know why he said he gave it to me? Why? Because *he* was sorry for *me*."

He stayed outside a long time, until he was so cold he felt he could never move a limb again. When he came back in, his father and mother had stopped crying and were calm again.

"At least I can get in the movies free, Dad," he said, and both of them broke out laughing. He sat on the arm of his father's chair.

"We're never going back to Jackson Street now, are we?" For a long time his father didn't answer him.

"No, we're never going back, boy," he said in an old, defeated voice.

"At last you're *both* growing up," his mother said.

He was growing up and he was very conscious of it. Growing up meant the power to go places and control things you couldn't before and it meant making your own chance to find a Jackson Street of your own. Now he knew he couldn't stay. Even though he loved them he knew his life with his family was over. The things he had grown accustomed to suddenly looked shabby and dingy and sad. There was a deeply repressed itching inside him to get up and begin to push around in the world.

Just a little less than a month later he started down the long slope to school but he never got there. In town he sold his bicycle for eight dollars and he took the train to Boston and from there to Providence and finally a bus to Valley Falls, Rhode Island.

The long walk from the main road to the walls of Our
Lady of the Valley Monastery filled him with expectation
and delight. It was April and the greenness of life was pressing out everywhere. He was convinced that the Lord was
directing him and sending him on a preordained mission.
He had no worry when the gate failed to open to his knock,
because it was said "Knock, and it shall be opened unto
you" and Father Desmarais said the Trappists never turned
away a knocker at the gate. A face finally appeared.

"Go away and come back later, my son. You are much too
young," the porter said. He wasn't dismayed. The next time
he pulled the bell cord hanging by the gate.

"I was told you never turned anyone away. I have come
to join you," he said.

"Stay there," the porter said. A very long time later, when
it was nearly dark, a different monk appeared and studied
him and beckoned him in. The monk held his fingers to his
lips and motioned Fred through the door. He shuffled down
into the dimness of the hall, and the boy, trembling with
inward elation, felt he was heading into the greatest adventure and mystery of his life.

6

"Now don't worry," Father Desmarais warned Fred's parents when they learned his whereabouts. "He has joined the most demanding religious order in the world and he'll be home in several weeks."

As the Trappists warn, no religious rule in the Western world at least demands more of its adherents. No order has stricter fasts, more complete rules on silence or demands harder labor. There is an obedience and a discipline for every moment of the day. The sheer dietary privation is rigorous enough to break all but the most determined. The Cistercians of Strict Observance never touch meat, or eggs, or fish. Although they produce some of the world's finest cheeses, it is a rare and festive occasion when they are allowed to touch it. A glass of milk is a supreme luxury.

The Trappist arises at 2:00 a.m., at which time he begins his day with spiritual contemplation and worship of God. At 5:30 he receives a breakfast of hard bread and crackers and a hot drink after which hard physical labor begins. At 11:30 the main meal of the day is served. On a harsh, winter day this feast is likely to consist of a small bowl of soup, a plate of two vegetables, three pieces of brown bread and a small bowl of fruit. After an afternoon of hard physical work and mental study a third scanty meal is served.

This, however, is not the most difficult of the Trappist ordeal. All of this privation is endured in absolute silence.

The need to talk for many men becomes a far greater obsession than food or privacy or sleep.

This mortification of the flesh is not meant to kill the human spirit or appetites but to rechannel them and ultimately to make the appetites disappear so that all desires become but one desire which is to know and bask and understand God's love so that the individual and that love become indivisible and one. This can only be done by intense contemplation and contemplation can only be achieved in silence.

Strangely and amazingly to those who knew him, Fred Demara endured. He loved it at Valley Falls. To his parents this was a stunning revelation as was the realization that their boy might someday become a priest—a man of the cloth.

Although he was eventually accorded the hooded robes and habit of the order and given the name Frater Mary Jerome, there were others in the order who were equally amazed. To the wise old men who sat and watched the smiling, eager novice was everything a contemplative should be except for his habits of contemplation. He didn't to them seem to be thinking anything but appeared, in fact, to be having the time of his life.

He was put in charge of two, big, half-trained mules and that was possibly a great mistake. One was named Lucifer and the other Luther, both bad actors and both typical of monastic humor at its best. There are rare times when a contemplative is permitted to talk and one of them is when it is essential in carrying out duties. It is well known that you can't handle balky mules by sign language.

The deep, sweet silence of the fields was continuously shattered by the roaring, joyous shouts of "Come on, Lucifer. Step lively there, boy. Gee, there, gee, boy," and other such vital talk. After an afternoon's work in the fields Frater M. Jerome's compulsion to talk was noticeably lessened. He was, in fact, usually hoarse.

It was an ancient story in life and in monasteries: "The spirit was willing but the flesh was weak."

"I was never more serious about anything in my life. I felt I had a deep, true devotion but I was a growing boy, a big growing boy, and at night when I lay down to think about God and His love I dreamt about bread and gravy and the love of it."

Once each day the monk is allowed more than the usual ration of bread if he feels it is vital. Fred began taking five and six pieces. One day, in jest, a brother left an entire three-foot-long loaf at Fred's place. It was meant to playfully embarrass him but it failed to do so. Using sign language he got off a memorable ploy:

"What? Only one piece of bread with my soup?"

After two years at Valley Falls, far longer than anyone ever expected the young man to last, the abbot and novice master had an earnest talk about their youngest novice and came to the agreement that, as fond of him as they were, he was simply not cut out for the silent life. They informed him of this and the boy was stung to the marrow of his being.

"I think it was the greatest hurt in my life," he says today.

There was an old monk he had befriended and he decided to stake everything on the monk's decision. If he thought he could make a contemplative he would request the right to stay and strive again. On the way over he plucked a flower and took it to the old man as a present. In the monk's cubicle he explained his dilemma and asked if he should stay.

"Oh no," said the old monk. "My heavens, no." The monk's eyes, which were smoky and sleepy-looking, were now bright and keen.

"You brought me that flower, didn't you? And you don't have permission to talk. And you're eating my cookies." He looked at the box.

"Almost all of them," he added drily. "Oh, I used to hear

you out in the fields shouting at those wonderful mules. What are their names?"

"Lucifer and Luther," Fred said, and his choked voice warned him he was closer to tears than he knew.

"Oh, how I liked to hear you. So full of life." The old man chuckled. "My only fear was that I was going to hear some real mule-skinner language and have to report it to the Chapter of Faults."

"I tried, Father. I did try," he sobbed.

"Oh, you did. I never gave you a week at first. But now you listen to me. There is room for more in the Church than the contemplatives. Have you ever studied a bishop's cross and wondered about it?"

He nodded that he had.

"Now, that cross is pointed at the bottom so that the bishop can goad the lazy. It's straight in the middle to support the weak. And it's bent at the top so he can hook the wanderers back into the fold. There is, in other words, plenty of room in our Church for a good mule driver."

He went to his desk and laboriously scratched out a note, which he folded and sealed in an envelope. "Now take this and when you leave, as you will, take it to the priest it is addressed to."

If there is one good thing about having no possessions in a monastery, it is that leaving poses no problem. Toward midnight, when he had cried out his shame at failure and shame was replaced by a certain anger at the way he had been treated after all he had done, he made his move to leave.

In an unlocked locker in a cellar he found his set of street clothes and then he went out across the quadrangle to the stable whose doors opened out into the back fields.

"Hey, boy, ho, boy." He untied the two drowsy beasts and led the sinners to the edge of the fields and there, with the stout handle of a cant hook, he whaled, as he puts it, "holy hell" out of the mules.

Whoever got those stubborn mules was going to have a hard time disciplining them again, he figured.

It didn't occur to him then that whoever got him next was going to have a hard time disciplining him.

When he came back from the stable, running along the shadows of the wall, a few lights were being turned on. Way across the fields he could hear one of the mules still braying in outraged anger and as he went up and over the low wall he decided that wasn't such a bad idea. He let out an ear-splitting whoop the likes of which have never been heard inside a Cistercian monastery probably before or since.

7

THE YOUNG CLERIC

He went home. His parents, who had been so hopeful for him, were disappointed but not unhappy. Father Desmarais had assured them that their boy had done amazingly well as it was. For several weeks he did nothing but eat and sleep, and by the time he had replenished his frame and slept untold hours of sleep he himself was amazed that he had survived as long as he had. He was happy that he had had the experience but as time moved him away from it he could not get over a conviction that he had somehow been cheated during it. He also, however, could not quite shake a feeling of shame and failure about it. He had gone to the very fountainhead of faith and been found lacking. What was left in him, for a variety of conflicting reasons, was a desire to someday show them—the Trappists—they were wrong.

Several weeks after leaving Valley Falls, while sitting in St. Laurence O'Toole's at Mass and wearing the same suit he had worn when he left, his hand felt the note the old monk had given him. His hand, he remembers, burned to open it. Later that morning he steamed it open over a tea kettle, the way he had seen it done in the movies, and what he read did not displease him.

The letter, addressed to the brother superior of the Brothers of Charity in Boston, was flattering. It stated that while he clearly was not a contemplative that he might have great value to the Church as an active religious who dealt with people. He had energy, a sense of humor, the instincts of a good politician and a sort of dedication to God.

"Every novice carries a bishop's miter in his tunic."

The thought was fantastic but who could ever forget that Cardinal O'Connell, the bishop of Boston, had come out of the mill blocks just up the river at Lowell? No one in Lawrence or Lowell. The sum of the letter was enough to send a thump of excitement spurting through his heart. For the first time he felt a surge of genuine ambition go through him. He left that night for Boston.

From the first day Demara was a standout as a novice. After the discipline of monastic life, his duties with the Brothers of Charity were almost like a vacation, and he had already mastered a solid body of basic Catholic dogma at Valley Falls. On finishing his novice training at Billerica, Massachusetts, as one of the brightest, he was immediately put to the stern test.

The Brothers of Charity are a service organization dedicated to supplying help and talent to undermanned Catholic institutions. They also run their own schools and several of their own institutions. Demara's first assignment was as a bottle washer and kitchen boy at Retreat St. Benoit, a Brothers of Charity home for aged, sick and disciplined priests on the outskirts of Montreal, where the order's headquarters were located. For a boy with visions of bishop's miters dancing in his head it was a dismal start.

The essence of charity is humility and in this one thing Brother John Berchmans, as he was named by the order, was deficient. No matter how hard he tried he could not rid himself of the feeling that compared to the Trappists the people he was with were only toying with religion. From the first bottle he washed to the last, he groaned with a sad indignation, a noise that didn't go unnoticed in the community. He had the conviction that to best serve his God he could be doing much better dispensing charity from a higher level.

He did, however, learn valuable things at the Retreat St.
Benoit. Almost all of the brothers there spoke French, and
Demara, in boredom, made an effort to learn it also. It was
to pay off handsomely later in his career. And then, put on
ward work, he had an unprecedented chance to see into the
interior soul of the organization of the Church. Many of the
priests there were men who had been sent for disciplinary
reasons to be rehabilitated, men with such problems as al-
coholism and dope addiction. A few of these were frankly
bitter men and some of these were eager to talk. They came
from many different organizations and backgrounds and
they told the eager boy with the exceptionally retentive
memory secrets about the workings of Church machinery
that many priests never discover or realize in a lifetime of
service. A cynical view of the fallibility and humanness of
the Church was revealed to him there and he never lost it.

"After what I learned and saw there, I never felt uneasy
in the presence of a bishop. I felt he was probably no better
than me but just disguised it better and had better connec-
tions," Demara since has said. He was to make use of his
attitude later.

On a night in April in 1941 he was called from his cubicle
to see the brother superior. In the room with the superior
were several other brothers, and Demara could see that the
visit was far from social. It looked, in fact, like a kangaroo
court. He listened in respectful silence while several brothers
attempted to explain the nature of their organization and
their concept of the word charity and he nodded that he
was, indeed, learning a lesson.

When he went back to his room, however, he didn't ponder his lecture in proper humility. He packed. He waited
until all was deep and tight in darkness and then he tiptoed
downstairs to the administration office, where he supplied
himself with a small cache of what he now calls "mad
money" and telephoned a taxi. When he saw the car's lights
outside he opened the door and took what the superior deli-

cately called French leave. He managed to catch the night train to Boston.

The next day Demara won his first organizational battle with the Church. He went directly to Billerica and told them how ill-adjusted he had been in Montreal. He had run into a wonderful but clannish bunch of French-Canadians whom he could not seem to join with and he had at times acted unwisely. Rather than bring up a sore point the brother at Billerica simply notified Montreal that their wandering Brother John was there and did they mind if he were reassigned. They did not. A few days later he was sent out as an instructor and guardian to Boyhaven, a Brothers of Charity home for boys in West Newbury, only fifteen miles from Lawrence.

It didn't take him long to find out what was wrong at Boyhaven. The plant itself was well enough run and the discipline was good but there wasn't enough love and fun going around. He was put in charge of the fourth grade and he determined, by following his rather original ideas of how to run a school, to make his grade the most outstanding class in the school.

"I don't know where I got those ideas about love and fun. I haven't the least memory of ever being exposed to them. I just knew when I got to Boyhaven that that was the way schools should be run. I haven't changed except that I would lay on the discipline with the love."

Instead of holding formal classes, Demara instituted little field trips and game times and storytelling periods. He took his class to see a stone quarry and a shoe factory and even the last operating textile plant in Lawrence. The brother superior was rankled. It was not that he objected to the program but that Brother Berchmans refused to discuss it with him before it was done.

With the aid of his parents Demara instituted a Bundles for Boyhaven program, and toys, clothes and money were collected. All of the bundles went to the fourth grade. One rare day in June, when heaven lay a particularly warm ear over the earth, the fourth grade pranced out of class in dashing new bathing suits to spend the afternoon in the sun under a sprinkler. The rest of Boyhaven was weak with envy.

"I'm going to have to ask you to tell your class to take off the swimming suits," Brother Superior said.

"I don't see why," Brother John said. He had been waiting for this. "Those suits were bought with money that was collected for me to be used by me."

"All monies go into the school fund for the general good of all the boys," the superior said heatedly.

"What general good?" Demara asked coolly, his eyes taking in the not luxurious surroundings.

"You will have those suits off those boys and the rest of that money in my office within ten minutes," the school head warned, "or you will receive the order's discipline. If you don't, I will see to it that you are sent out of the Brothers of Charity."

"So I have ten minutes?" he said. "If you're going to take that attitude why should I do what you say?"

It was the same case as with the Trappists, he felt. There was no question that he was giving his all. There was no denying that grade four was the best grade in the school. It was another case where his talents and efforts were not appreciated by an authority jealous of his energy and success. There was also no denying that there was little excess of love between the two men.

"He was a true Brother of Charity," Demara has since described the superior. "Tight with a buck and hard as nails."

In turn, a recent inquiry about Demara's career at Boyhaven drew this response in full.

"We have nothing to say and we don't want to have anything to do with that man."

He went to his room and packed. As he came back across the sweltering lawn to the main house, smiling at the sight of his boys still romping and shouting under the sprinkler, he passed the school station wagon and could not help noticing the keys to it dangling from the lock. He had never really driven any car before, but he had the most certain idea that he would find out how as soon as he tried. He opened the door away from the main house as quietly as possible, put his bag in the front seat, managed without too much noise to get the motor started and then, in a manner he wasn't sure about, managed to get it going forward. He assumed that he would learn how to drive the car and stop it on the way, and he did.

He went to New Hampshire and then turned back down toward Boston, driving through Lawrence as he did, and that night he parked the car in a parking lot next to North Station in Boston and then went to dinner at the Olde Union Oyster House, a place he had often heard his father mention when he was very young. He bought all the papers and with a sudden, strange thrill he began reading the story of his escapade.

It was quietly and decidedly and deeply exhilarating, he found, to sit in a famous restaurant, casually eating oysters, heady with the smell of wine and smoke and food and women, to look at those around you and cherish the secret of yourself. He suddenly felt completely in command of things.

He ordered the first drink of his life and was very nearly transported by it. When he reached the street again, despite the steamy heat that clung to the town, he felt like dancing down it. Instead of doing that, at the top of Corn Hill Road near Scollay Square, on an impulse, in a flippant, devilish mood, he went into a little recruiting booth and enlisted in the United States Army.

8

THE SOLDIER

The very next morning, after having been stripped of mufti and popped into khaki, he realized he had made a serious mistake. The Army life was not for him. He had nothing in common with it or with the men in it.

Many of the men before Pearl Harbor were either professional soldiers, drifters who couldn't find or wouldn't hold a job, or a handful of bitter draftees who held the idea that they had been legally shanghaied. Their cry was OHIO which, translated, meant Over the Hill in October. He was shocked by the language he heard and by the morals and manners of the men. He hated most of all the public latrines, where men were forced to relieve themselves in full view of others. He wasn't by nature a prude by any means; it was just that the monastic life had been poor basic training for the military life.

He also was ashamed of his ignorance about such things as sex and the cruder ways of the world, and to hide his ignorance he avoided all bull sessions dealing with such subjects, with the result that he got the reputation for being a "saint" which he deplored. When he was shipped out of Camp Devens for basic training at Keesler Field Air Force Base in Biloxi, Mississippi, he determined, with this fresh chance, to become a "real wise guy." It is to his credit as a character manipulator that he succeeded beyond even his expectations.

"I had never done anything like it before. I was mad at

the Army just because I was in it. When I got to Keesler—oh, *there* was a dump in those days—I simply sat down and began studying the Army organization and probed around for loopholes. You know the Army—there were millions of them. I really amazed myself at the cold-blooded way I went about it. Me, just a boy from the monasteries."

Keesler was then in the process of being built and was an enormous tent city, sprawling on the fringe of a dismal, moss-covered, steaming swamp over the remains of a beat-up turpentine plantation. Of all the ghastly daily chores at Keesler the worst was the chow line. There was only one mess tent and troops lined up for hours in the broiling sun for their chance to eat in the roasting mess tent. If you failed to faint on line, you had an even chance to succeed once you got inside. It is possibly legend but one of the survivors of the Bataan Death March, when asked how he managed to survive, answered simply, "I received my training on the mess line at Keesler."

Demara conquered the mess line. He noted that Keesler was constantly shipping people to other bases at almost any time of the day or night. Shipping clerks were armed with little blue arm bands to identify them and invariably carried rolls of mimeographed shipping orders. It was quite simple to look like a shipping clerk, he found. It was equally simple, decked out as he was, to start at the tag end of the almost endless line of sufferers and shout, "Carruthers? Private Quentin Q. Carruthers? Rush shipping orders!" and in this fashion move his way up, up, the terrible long line until he reached the door of the mess tent, which was guarded by several military policemen, and run shouting in. At the head of the line he would pocket his papers, produce a mess kit from under his shirt and proceed to load it up with food. There is every good chance that he would have been lynched by the men had he ever gotten caught.

It is his boast that he never actually pulled one full day of duty in the Army. The night before his unit was to pull

KP he would leave his bed made up and after lights were out sleep under it. When the KP chaser came early in the morning Demara would roll out from under and pretend to be coming back from the latrine.

"Where's this guy?" the chaser would ask of the only man handy to reply.

"Poor chap," he would say. "Name's Demara. Emergency leave. His mother is dying in Kansas." The name Demara would be crossed off the roster. They never, as Fred suspected, bothered to check back. He would spend the rest of his day sleeping in the shade.

He spent his free time, of which he had considerable, developing similar stratagems to cover every conceivable military situation.

Somewhere along the way he had also developed a highly personal version of Thomas Locke's social contract philosophy which, for those who have forgotten it, goes, roughly: If the individual in a society can't go along with the rules of that society then the individual reserves for himself the right to withdraw from that society. He is a part of society as a result of his freely made contract with it, and he can at any time declare the contract null and void.

Demara decided that his contract with the Army had come to an end. He had no qualms about quitting; his only care was doing it right. Rightness came in the form of one Anthony Ingolia, a tentmate at Keesler.

Ingolia now explains their friendship, "I thought he was the funniest man in the world. Of all the gold bricks he was the champion. I was just a kid from New Orleans but he had been around. Then when I learned he was a defrocked priest, man, I was really impressed and scared even. You wonder why I believed him? One morning on the way to my mother's house he stopped the car in some small town and he asked the priest there to let him serve Mass and he did it. I didn't know how to take that man after that."

Demara knew how to take him. One night in New Orleans on a week-end pass Ingolia's proud mother produced from Anthony's room a solid wooden box. In it were all the mementos and records of his life.

"I was embarrassed when she dug them out. I thought Demara was going to die from boredom. 'Gee, Mom,' I said, 'put 'em away. He's my friend and you're going to kill him.' I was amazed. He just sat there going over and over those things until even my mother got tired of them."

" 'Whattaya' see in those things?' I asked him."

" 'Life,' he said. 'I see a whole life ahead of me.' "

Several weeks later the time was right. The trainees were scheduled to take a long night march. Demara filed down an angry blister on his heel with some sandpaper and got himself excused. The troops were excused from duty until the next afternoon, so he had a minimum of eighteen hours before being checked. He packed a little bag and armed with a fraudulent pass, of which he had plenty, he walked out of Keesler, thumbed a ride to Biloxi and took a bus to New Orleans. Mrs. Ingolia was surprised, indeed, to see the friend of her son at the door of her house that evening. She was as flattered as the first time when he asked to go over Anthony's records again, and when she went up to bed he was still sitting downstairs going over his friend's old school yearbooks. He was such a nice boy. When she got up in the morning he had left a charming note thanking her for her hospitality, and the box was back in Anthony's room, safely locked again. It was just as well that she didn't open it since there was almost nothing left in it and she would only have worried.

Fred Demara was now in possession of all of Anthony Ingolia's credentials.

It is reasonable to ask why he did it. His reasoning is serenely simple. He was wanted for car theft in Massachusetts. His career in the Army was intolerable and impossible. He had a determination to be useful, he says, and to do good

again, but he couldn't reënter the Church, the place where
he could be most useful and do the most good, under his
own name. Since his aim was to do good, anything he did to
do it was justified. With Demara the end *always* justifies
the means. Stealing Ingolia's papers was not in itself a bad
act if he didn't do bad things with them. It was, in fact, a
good act. Demara has always been blessed with a very personal conception of God looking down, reading the motives
in his head, and nodding approvingly. With that picture
in his mind he knew little shame and less fear.

There is one other thing that should be known since it
plays a very important part in Demara's career. There is in
the Roman Catholic Church a procedure known as letter of
testimony. This is the Church's own rudimentary security
check. If a person wishes to enter a religious order, a letter
requesting a letter of testimony is sent to the diocese in
which the person was baptized and in which he was confirmed and in which he spent at least one calendar year as
a Catholic. This is first a courtesy since the bishop of the
person's baptismal area always has first call on that person's services (a courtesy almost never used), and second a
simple police check. Through it the Church learns if a person
hasn't been baptized or confirmed or has already piled up a
sordid record in the Church or the world.

The system is fairly effective. A check on Demara's letter
of testimony, at that time, would have revealed that he had
been asked to leave the Cistercians, had fled one Brothers
of Charity organization and robbed another. It would have
been enough not only to keep him out of the Church's service
but to put him in jail.

As Anthony Ingolia, however, Demara presented an entirely different picture. A check on Ingolia would simply
bring confirmation of the fact that Ingolia had indeed been
baptized and confirmed in New Orleans and had no other
record. This might seem over simple, but the Church does
not function as a detective agency and also doesn't assume

that thieves and the like are going to falsify their way into
monasteries and religious orders.

All of this Demara had learned from the priests at the
retreat in Montreal. His past was beginning to pay off.

The morning after he took the documents he went to the
New Orleans Public Library and consulted the Catholic
Directory, an enormous compendium of Catholic information, listing all the priests, all the dioceses and orders of the
Church. He found what he wanted. It was the mother house
of them all, the purest of the pure, the Abbey of Our Lady
of Gethsemani, the Trappist monastery later made famous
by Thomas Merton in his book *The Seven Storey Mountain.*

Compared to Gethsemani, Valley Falls, he felt, was bush
league. He would show them. With a high heart and a feeling of sincere devotion he took a train to Louisville,
Kentucky (covered by a legal-looking but fabricated traveling order he had had the foresight to steal at Keesler), where
he bought a civilian suit for $10 in a second-hand store and
dumped his Army garb, and proceeded by bus, out to Trappist, Kentucky, where the great monastery was located.
For reasons that will be plain later Gethsemani will not be
described here. Let it go for the moment that hardly one
week had passed when he felt a tugging on his sleeve and
turned, with a sickening start, to look into the eager, smiling face of a younger monk who had transferred to Gethsemani from Valley Falls. Demara had the good sense and
the cold blood not to show any sign of recognition. He looked
at the man, in fact, as if he were slightly crazy but that was
the end. A few hours later he asked for the return of his
clothes and when he got them he took his walk up the long,
poplar-lined road leading out to the highway.

He was very sad. He felt he loved Gethsemani, and as he
looked back at it from out on the highway he made a vow
that somehow he was going to come back to it someday.

"I meant that vow. Maybe I still do. But I went about it
in a pretty dumb way. I was hurt and back in love with

the Cistercians, so I took what money I had and lit out for the Trappist monastery called New Melleray. That's in Iowa, just outside of Des Moines."

His major worry at New Melleray was that when they got testimonial on Ingolia, they would find it soiled. They would find he had left Gethsemani under sudden circumstances and he was quite sure that would hurt him. That problem was somewhat helped, however, by the fact that all abbey mail was placed in cubbyholes easily accessible to the young novice Demara. He knew this much: any green letter (which signifies a letter from a bishop's office) bearing a New Orleans stamp would be about him.

When the letter did come in, it was worse than he had expected. They had not only traced Ingolia's path back to Gethsemani but had assumed that one Fred W. Demara was the man using his name. It seems that Mrs. Ingolia's parish priest had complimented her one Sunday on Anthony's entering the Trappists, and the inevitable and obvious investigation had followed. When the wooden box was opened it was found to be empty.

"As the song says, I packed my duds and made my getaway. For all I know they never did get any testimonial letter and they must still be wondering whatever happened to that prize novice Ingolia."

That should have been the end of Ingolia but it wasn't. While thumbing a ride to St. Louis he heard the news about Pearl Harbor and had a feeling that he had to get home to Lawrence. His life was taking a turn he couldn't control, he felt, and what with the war he thought he'd better get home and start again. But he needed money. Most people would have holed up in a YMCA and wired, but not Demara. In St. Louis he presented himself as a candidate for the seminary of the Passionist Fathers and then wrote home. His only worry was one of time, whether the answer to his letter home would come first or the letter from New Orleans on this candidate Ingolia. The letter from Lawrence won. A week before Christmas, Demara left all of his Ingolia papers stacked in his cubicle, put on his $10 suit and took the train for Boston. The career of Anthony Ingolia, a very minor first attempt, was over. Demara arrived in Lawrence two days before Christmas and a week after the last military policeman had made a search of the house.

It was not a happy Christmas. His father, an ardent patriot as is Demara, could not bring himself to speak to his son.

"There's only one answer, son," his father finally said. "You've got to go back and face the music and take your medicine like a man. You'll get out from behind bars soon enough, believe me, and then you'll have a clean slate."

For all his cynicism about many things he felt miserable about hiding out in Lawrence for the duration of the war.

"You can put this down," he says. "I wanted to . . . these are the words . . . 'do my part.' I didn't want to miss the big experience of my generation. And I like this country, you know. Where else but in America could a man do all I've done? *That's* what I call freedom."

It is an odd point but well taken.

"All right, Dad," he said one morning, "I'm ready now. I'm going down to Boston and turn myself in."

With the freshness that characterizes much of his thinking, however, Demara, on the way down, decided that he could do himself and his country a lot more good by fulfilling his patriotic duties outside of jail. In Boston he continued on to New York and settled the problem. Under the name of Fred W. Demara he enlisted in the Navy.

9

War or no war, he hated it. After eight miserable weeks in boot camp he was at once assigned to the USS *Ellis,* a destroyer operating on the North Atlantic run. Life on a destroyer is for a man who finds the sea a thrilling though stern challenge. Demara is not this kind. Braving the icy, mountainous waves and the German submarine wolf packs on the Iceland route were to him an agonizing, sometimes frightening, monumental bore. He began a massive campaign to get himself accepted to Hospital School and his letters were so frequent, urgent and annoying that he actually succeeded.

He hadn't known he had any interest in medicine, but he liked it at once. In the school he studied hard and he did well. For probably the first time in his life he studied the things he was supposed to study, was put on the honor roll and wasn't in the least surprised to find that, when he wanted to be, he was an excellent and quick student. After graduating from the basic course he at once applied for advanced training. His request was turned down flat. The reason given was that he did not have a proper or adequate educational background.

The rejection stunned him. "I went around as if someone had hit me right between the eyes. Here I scored the highest on all the tests and because someone had a couple of years in college they picked him and kicked me out."

Instead they sent him out as a medical corpsman to a Marine beach battalion where he spent his time slogging around in the boondocks of Virginia near Norfolk with a bunch of Marines playing at war. The thing to do, it occurred to him one steamingly hot afternoon as they labored up the side of a shifting, unrelenting sand dune, was to *get* the proper background. Once that problem was presented the only remaining problem was how. The solution just happened to him. "Not that I wasn't looking for it," Demara adds.

He was sitting in a serviceman's club musing on his low estate when a sailor next to him left his seat. On it lay a booklet—a catalog from the Iowa State College at Ames, Iowa. Demara began flipping idly through it when it occurred to him that everyone in that book had what he needed. Some of the people had whole little clusters of academic honors stringing along behind their names like glittering jewels.

"I hadn't had much experience in life but I knew that those little letters automatically gave those people—and I don't care how dumb some of them might have been—prestige and positions of authority," Demara explains. "Because of them people automatically became officers and gentlemen, and then because of a lack of them some really brilliant people were forced to remain enlisted men."

And the old Demara philosophy was operating. If you were able to perform well the job you would get then it really didn't matter how you got the job. If the end result would be good, that is all that mattered.

"Even as a patriotic gesture, so I could contribute more than I was, I felt I had better steal some academic credits."

He went back to his bunk to ponder the problem. The very first thing he figured—a factor which has since played heavily in all his plans—was that he would need some good-looking, formal, official stationery.

In any operation or caper Demara's basic strategy is to make the open, obvious and daring move. "Like the famous Marshal Foch who my father admired. 'My left is under attack, my right is crumbling, the center can not hold. Excellent—I attack.' That's my theory, too, only when I was younger I overdid it."

He asked the captain in command of his base for a private meeting about a highly personal matter, and, after much wrangling, permission was granted. As Demara suspected, on the captain's desk was a neat pile of stationery and next to the desk a gray metal wastebasket.

"Sir," he began, talking in a low, rather mysterious voice, "I have information that I felt should only be released to you personally."

While talking he pulled out a cigarette and proceeded to light it with a match he had soaked in kerosene and then coated with wax. It was not really a match but a midget torch. This, when it was flaming well, he tossed into the wastebasket.

The sum of his mysterious information was that he suspected some of the officers' wives were abusing their food commissary privileges. He never did finish his exposé, however.

"FIRE!" he roared. "FIRE, FIRE, FIRE!" In the process of panicking, he managed to kick the flaming basket over so that the captain's rug began to burn in patches.

"GET A FIRE EXTINGUISHER!" Demara roared, and true to his expectations the captain made a rush for the hall. Demara made a lean for the desk. In the excitement he managed to stuff the front of his middy blouse with stationery and envelopes.

The odor of burned wool and melted paint was still heavy in the air when Seaman Demara attempted to go on with his story.

"Captain," he said. "Believe me. You can't imagine how sorry I am for setting fire to your office but . . ."

It was the captain's turn to attack.

"GET OUT!" he shouted. "Get out of this office or I'll break every bone in your overstuffed body. I will personally . . ."

But the sailor never heard the rest. He was on his feet and moving fast toward the door. A week later, in fact, he was transferred to a new unit entirely, a fact which made his plan all the more effective.

From the Iowa State catalog he picked the name of a man who possessed reasonable credentials and who also was on leave to the Navy. His first step was, on regular stationery, to write the registrar at Ames telling them that he was being considered for an important and sensitive new post in the Navy and asking how to go about getting a transcript of his grades. If his request was all right, he went on, would they please send them either to himself or to Captain T. D. Canfield in care of Naval Security Placement Board at the following address. The address happened to be that of a local gas station where Demara had paid a dollar for the privilege of using it as a mail drop and pick-up.

This is what he calls the "innocent bumpkin" opening. You ask such simple, naïve questions that a person would have to have an especially dismal view of humanity to figure that this was the first step in chicanery.

The next day he followed his bumpkin letter with what he calls "official paper." On the stationery stolen from the captain he put through a letter to the registrar asking for (demanding would be closer to it) a transcript of the man's grades. They could be sent to the candidate himself, to the Navy Security Placement Board or to the captain himself, whatever was the correct procedure. The captain's address was, of course, the gas station. During this time he had had made a small rubber stamp saying Security Placement Board, Temp. Offices and the same address. Stamping this on a piece of routine Navy stationery Demara then sent another request for grades but added that if a request had already been received to please ignore this one. The letter wound up apologizing for any duplication of effort but explained that the rapid development of the Navy base made such errors understandable.

"This is known as 'papering in advance,'" Demara explains. "It makes it easy for the person being requested to comply. By the time you make the actual pitch they aren't surprised, they are sitting around waiting for it."

A set of transcripts arrived a few days later at the gas station and as of that moment the Security Placement Board went out of operation. He was not an expert at handling documents. At that time his sole actual knowledge was gleaned from a Johnson and Smith catalog called something like *How to Be a Private Detective and Earn BIG Money*.

Demara rented a cheap room in a rundown Norfolk hotel and went to work doctoring his papers. His system was crude. He had tried erasing and using ink remover and found that to be impossible. He next rented a typewriter and typed his name and other relevant information on plain white paper and then cut them out in thin strips and pasted these on top of the real information on the document. As an example: where it said Place of birth—Waterloo, Iowa, Demara pasted over Lawrence, Mass. At the bottom of the document he pasted an official-looking seal he had bought in a dime store and under it he wrote: *Certified copy. Original records must be held.* To this he added the signature of the Iowa State registrar which he had cut off the bottom of the answering letter accompanying the transcripts. When this was all together he took the sheets downtown and had the whole mass photostated several times. The finished product represented a sound-looking package. The documents looked so good (he had added a few extra courses which he felt would look good for a Navy man to have in his background) that he decided instead of asking to go to advance medical school he would quite rightly apply for a commission. He showed his credentials to several officers he knew and they were impressed. They were glad to write covering letters to the effect that they felt this seaman was worthy of consideration for an officer's commission. The whole bundle of documents with covering letters was then duly deposited with the board of officers in Norfolk who review applications for officer candidates.

He was told there would be a delay of several weeks before a decision was made and he resigned himself to it. During the wait he began a most interesting hobby. He had found it a cunning and intriguing game, fooling bureaucracy. Using the tricks he had worked on Iowa, he set out to perfect his crude techniques and to collect the credentials of a whole host of people. He sent away for various college catalogs and set to work with enthusiasm.

"Just the children of an idle brain," he says.

It thrilled him each day to pay a visit to his mail drop and see what illegal, odd documents the postman brought. He felt he was a kind of mastermind thief; the people he was robbing *sent* him the loot he wanted, at their expense.

A choice project became one Dr. Robert Linton French.

"Why did I choose French?" he once asked. "For one thing I liked the name. It is French and yet, oddly, unmistakably English and I felt it suited me. For another, French offered me a real challenge. I'd have a real job to mine all his academic nuggets."

French was a graduate of Michigan, where he had also earned his master's degree, was a Ph. D. from Stanford and had been Research Fellow at Yale.

"Besides, I have *always* been willing to bask in the glory of a Ph. D."

Also during this time he got leave and went home to Lawrence. His family were more than a little astonished to find their son in a sailor suit, but Fred managed to put them at ease. He had gone back and "faced the music and taken his medicine" he assured them and now he was still attached to the Army but was on a rather special assignment with the Navy. No one could say he was lying about that.

While he was home he staked himself outside the parish rectory one afternoon until he saw the pastor leave and drive away, and then he brazenly, without ringing, walked into the rectory office and began picking up every kind of stationery and document he could. He got baptismal and confirmation certificates and wedding papers and on these he began imprinting the parish seal. He didn't stop when he found an old lady, the rectory housekeeper, eyeing him.

"How *does* this thing work, Mother?" he asked gaily. "Amazing little device." That was the rule of Foch coming into play. Always attack.

When he saw her eyeing the small pile of documents and he noted that she was about to reach for them, he backed clumsily into a bottle of holy water which was resting on a table nearby. "Oh, dear," he said as it shattered on the marble floor. While the housekeeper went for a mop he sealed some more documents and stuffed them under his middy blouse.

"Will you tell the pastor I had a priceless visit?" Demara said.

"I'll tell him that if it's the like of you that's defendin' this country, then God help the nation," she said bitterly.

Demara has since realized that she was the first person to suspect he was a fraud.

On his way back to Norfolk he stayed over in Boston and did a thing that still astonishes him. On what he insists was purely an impulse he presented himself at Cardinal O'Connell's residence in Boston and announced himself as Dr. Robert Linton French. On the basis of his title he gained an audience with the cardinal. Even in a seaman's suit, as Dr. French he found he was *somebody*. The conversation was simply that of a courtesy nature but he found himself talking smoothly and easily, the way he never could have done as himself.

On the way out he smoothly and easily managed to filch several pages of the cardinal's red stationery although he didn't manage a single envelope.

At Norfolk people were waiting for him. There was no question about getting a commission. The only question was one of how the Navy personnel people had managed to miss him.

"I see nothing to hold us back here," an officer said at a first hearing. "After routine security check-outs I think we'll be happy to give you a commission."

"I, ah, don't really *have* any background to check," Demara said weakly.

"Anyone with an educational record like this," the officer said, tapping the phony transcripts, "has a background. A splendid background."

Splendid, indeed, Demara thought. He had far overplayed his hand. He went back to his quarters and did the only possible thing. He packed his little handbag.

"I could see that my usefulness to the service was o'er," he says.

He waited until the covering darkness of evening and went out along the Navy docks where, at the end of a pier, he left a set of Navy clothes and a hat with his name printed in it and a note which went: "I have made a fool of myself. This is the only way out. Forgive me. F. W. Demara."

"It was rather simple, wasn't it, but it might have worked. It was worth the try. As far as I was concerned, F. W. Demara was dead. My only regret was that I had but two or three lives to give for my country."

He went back into Norfolk where he bought a civilian suit and where he bought several other things. One was an honorable discharge and the other was a false officer's identification card (these were for sale in Norfolk then) with his own face and fingerprints on the card. Then he started out of Norfolk, thumbing westward by night, with a whole fresh life ahead. As he waited out on the road he thought over his handling of things in Norfolk and realized that he had blundered badly, especially on aspects of psychology.

"And that, of course, was just ridiculous," he now explains. "I mean, me being a Ph. D. in psychology."

For Demara was dead, drowned in the oily waters of Norfolk. He was now Dr. Robert Linton French, doctor of psychology and de-commissioned officer in the U. S. Navy, at anyone's service.

10

As Dr. French went westward an old unrequited love returned to burn in Demara's bosom. Almost irresistibly he found his path leading back to Gethsemani. With Dr. French's elaborate credentials he was bound to get some kind of preferential treatment, he felt. He had little to fear from anyone who might step up and say "Aren't you the monk who used to be back at Valley Falls?"

The proper answer was "No, I'm not, but I pity the poor soul who looks like me."

To succeed, all impostors must sooner or later learn and have confidence that the burden of proof is always on the accuser. In Demara's case, unless someone had virtually the facilities of a police department on hand, his chances of proving that he was *not* Dr. French and had been at Valley Falls were not very good.

At Gethsemani Demara presented himself at the portal as Dr. Robert L. French, a man who had experienced the futility of war and who desired to become a contemplative. Even in a place as simple, and thus as sophisticated, as Gethsemani having a man with a Ph. D. apply for admission to your organization has effect. He was taken directly to the abbot, the Right Reverend Frederick Dunne, who was impressed by the convert's background and very apparent sincerity. Until he could be baptized he was confined to Visitors' Quarters but when that was done he was allowed to enter the novitiate.

The monastic life, after the softness of the Army and Navy,

was much harder than he had imagined or remembered it to be. Worst of all was the silence, and this time he didn't have two recalcitrant mules as talking buddies.

Even harder was the novitiate training. He had gone through it once and Demara, not unexpectedly, has the kind of mind that thrives on variety. He did amaze the old monks by his ability to learn. When the Trappists are at services each brother has in front of him a huge songbook in which, in elaborate script, is all of the Gregorian plain song that makes up the litany of the day. It takes some men years to learn the contents of their book. The sign of a rookie is his need for a light behind him. The old hands sit in darkness. After several weeks Demara one evening reached up and switched off his light. The novice master came down and put it back on. After a short time Demara again turned it off. When an irate novice master again passed by, Demara showed by sign language, which is the monk's way of talking, that he had memorized the contents of his book. This was naturally greeted with a certain amount of incredulity, that a convert should walk in and master the ritual in what would amount to hours. The next day he showed them that he had indeed done just that. That night he sat in darkness and the old monks, into whose eyes his light had shone, were thankful. They also were amazed.

Mainly, however, he was eager, as Dr. French, to get on with the work his degrees entitled him to perform. Deeply buried in the back of his mind was the ambition to become the voice to the outside world for all contemplatives. Here are some of the titles for projected papers he wrote down at the time:

Diet and Its Effects on the Devotional Community

"On this I was an expert. I thought I could bring my whole mind and stomach to bear on the problem."

Results of Continued Continence on Contemplatives

Of Monks and Men: Spiritual Man in Materialistic Society

"I knew exactly where to crib for this one. Coming from a monastery like Gethsemani it could have been spectacular, I think."

He had no fear that he could not carry out his plans. "I was Dr. French, that's all. As Dr. French I felt I could do these things and I could have done them."

Two years, the time of the novitiate service, is long indeed for a person of wavering faith, a fact the Trappists are well aware of. The first corrosion in Demara's spiritual armor was created by hunger. The sight of a horse munching grass disturbed him and the sight of a finch eating pumpkin seeds filled him with envious rage. He began dreaming about food at night and, finally, filching it by day.

The Trappists have a ritual known as the Chapter of Faults, an ordeal at which members of the community admit their faults, and, in rare cases, members are forced to disclose other member's sins. At first Demara admitted his transgressions regarding food, but they became so many that he finally chose silence. Late in his first autumn Demara was assigned to work in their now extinct vineyards with another brother who turned out to have as little will power as Demara. They recognized each other with that sure instinct that they say one con man working an area recognizes another con man. By the end of their first day the two not only were talking breathlessly while huddled over, mulching the roots of the vines, they were eating the grapes as well.

It was almost inevitable, since the grapes had to be eaten while crouching over, that some of the juice would dribble out and down onto the white habit Brother Mary Jerome—that was his Gethsemani name—wore. A great purple stain spread out across the top of his habit.

"Then I knew how Hester Prynne must have felt in the *Scarlet Letter*," Demara says. "Everywhere I went people stared at me shamelessly because everyone knew grapes hadn't been on the menu since last autumn."

It was his red badge of discouragement, his own scarlet

letter plastered on his chest for all to read. No amount of washing could out the damn spot.

Whenever he entered the Chapter of Faults there was nothing for him to do but drop to the floor, as is the proper posture, and disparage himself.

"I had a fear that I was losing my devotion fast, though," Demara says. "Every time I was down there instead of praying for humility and courage to resist temptation I was figuring out how I could eat those grapes the next week and not leave a stain."

There were other matters. He was caught talking constantly. Finally his partner in debasement went before the Chapter of Faults and detailed his association with Frater Mary Jerome.

"I could have murdered that saintly bum. He was cleansing his own soul, all right, but he was sending me down the road to ruin doing it."

After those revelations there was nothing to do but seize the initiative. He arranged a hearing with Abbot Dunne. The sum of his conversation was that his stay at Gethsemani had been immensely informative but that he realized he could best serve the Church in more active fashion.

"I am glad that you came to that conclusion, Doctor," the abbot said, not without what sounded like a threat in his voice. Despite his apparent disapproval of the doctor's career with the Trappists, however, he did write a short, rather noncommittal note introducing Demara to whatever order he next might try.

"If I were you I'd try the Benedictines, Brother," he was told by a novice also soon to leave. "You're an intellectual and when it comes to the intellectuals the Bennies are right up front leading the parade. As for physical labor, if you don't want it, the worst you might have is some leaf raking. It's sort of a monastic WPA, you might say."

Specifically he had been alerted to the New Subiaco Abbey, an order of American Cassinese (from the Monte

Cassino abbey in Italy), and stemming from the Swiss Benedictines. The abbey was situated deep in the Ozark Mountains of Arkansas.

As he started down the poplar-lined road he had a jaunty, expectant feeling but while he waited for a car or bus to come he watched a group of novitiates and monks working in perfect harmony and peace in the fields and a wave of indescribable sadness swept over him.

He had a feeling that this was the end of his Cistercian career. He was a failure. Worse than that, he was scum.

"At that moment I would have auctioned the rest of my life for the courage to turn around and walk back down that road and confess my whole story to Abbot Dunne and begin again."

He feels today that he was about to do that when the devil, in the guise of a Kentucky hill farmer, came instead.

"Get on, mister," the dirty, lank man said. The back of the pick-up truck was rich with the sweet stench of manure. "Always room for more," the man said.

"Where are you headed for?" Demara asked.

"New Hope," the farmer answered, and Demara burst into laughter. "It was all so fitting and appropriate. A load of manure and me, the excrement of the world, going down the road for New Hope."

He climbed aboard and they began jangling down the road.

"Poor boys, cain't even have a drink," the man said. "You was one of them, huh? Here," he said. He handed Demara a fruit jar filled with clear liquid. "Take a pull on this. Make you feel right with the world."

It was hot and it was blinding but it was also good. It was popskull, white lightning, that ol' mountain dew, the good raw moonshine whiskey of the mountains. By the time they reached New Hope, the Canaan for his salvation, both men were gloriously, roaringly and beautifully drunk.

When he awoke the next morning he was spread-eagled

on the hump of the dung-hill in the truck. He lay for a moment trying to open his eyes against the golden swarm of the sun on his lids. What had gone before was forgotten, and although his head hurt, he could feel the warm of the sun and hear the whirr of insects and smell the realness of the richness he was planted in.

This was the bottom, he thought, a new low. But he couldn't make himself feel bad about it.

"Hey, buddy," someone said, shaking him. "You all right? What you doin' up there?"

"Don't worry about me," Demara said. "I'm gettin' up now because I can't go down."

Suddenly the world was a place of infinite possibilities again.

"If you dare to go out and try to get what you want, you can get it," he said half aloud, as he wiped clots of dung from off his clerical garb.

11

From New Hope, Demara went to Little Rock where he began "papering" himself at New Subiaco. He did a thorough
job. By the time he arrived he fully expected to be met at the
bus stop by a welcoming committee and part of the school
band.

He had prepared for his arrival by presenting the letter
from Abbot Dunne (real), a letter on red cardinal's stationery
from Cardinal O'Connell of Boston (false) and a glowing
personal letter from the priest in Lawrence written on the
stationery he had stolen (also false). These would not be
likely to be checked, but then Demara, to hasten his confirmation into the Church (he was a convert and hadn't been
confirmed at Gethsemani) filled out a confirmation certificate which he had lifted back in Lawrence and signed it
Right Reverend Francis J. Spellman, who, of course, is
now Cardinal Spellman.

"I have always found that it pays to use the biggest names.
People are reluctant to bother important people on routine
matters. And they don't expect a fraud to use such obvious
names."

The danger was that in the process of getting a letter of
testimony for French, the documents would be returned to
Lawrence where the parish priest, if he looked too hard at
the documents, might get the idea that they were forgeries.

The monastery ran a rather large, good boys' school, and
while awaiting the start of yet another novice training, Dr.

French was assigned as a science teacher. His old ideas had not changed. The doctor seemed to lean toward the "bull session" theory of lecturing, the sessions well larded with anecdotes and jokes.

On November 17, 1943, the testimonial letter was issued through the archdiocese of Boston by the Right Reverend John Wright clearing French's forged documents, and several days after that the papers were returned to Demara. That really took the wraps off the new professor. Cleared and safe, with fresh letter of testimony, Dr. French decided to liven up the state of education at New Subiaco. His light could be seen burning late into the night as he read ahead on the next day's material to stay a day ahead of his classes and as he salted and peppered his lectures with comedy material and shafts of wit.

The only thing that was suffering was his novitiate training, but it was difficult for the novice master to press him on that point. He seemed to know all the answers. The one important fact that he didn't know was that on December 3, the Right Reverend Paul Nahlen, abbot of New Subiaco, received a phone call from Right Reverend Wright calling back Cardinal O'Connell's letter of testimony. It would seem that the Reverend Edmund Daley in Lawrence, after tossing and turning late into one night about something that bothered him and wouldn't let his mind alone, suddenly sat up in bed and realized that it was the documents he had okayed. He wanted a second look at them and, on second thought, so did Boston.

Dr. French was asked, with no explanation, to return his papers to the abbot's office and he turned them in with vague misgivings.

"What's this all about?" he asked.

"I'm afraid I can't tell you that," the abbot's assistant said.

He was angry about it. He had won the first moves in the game and now the other side wanted to play all over again after losing.

"I felt it really was galling. Why did they want to keep checking me anyway? Look at it this way. Here was this little cluster of clerics sipping from the Pierian springs—in Arkansas, mind you—and a kind providence sends them a Ph.D.—in psychology, mind you—and what do they do? They start a campaign to kill the goose that just might lay them some golden eggs," he has said. He looked down on the Phi Beta Kappa key he generally sports.

"I don't think a doctor of philosophy had ever even driven through the place before I got there. And one probably hasn't since," he mused. "Disgraceful performance!"

In the weeks that followed he was constantly nervous, conscious of being under observation. His Christmas and New Year's, he says, were ruined and he began drinking to put himself in a more cheerful frame of mind. Several times he blacked out and once he passed out on the far edge of the football field and might have frozen to death if a rabbit hunter hadn't found him.

As January wore on and nothing happened, he began to become his old self once again until on the mid-morning of January 10, he was summoned from one of his classes to Abbot Nahlen's office. He was set for what he might face. As he crossed the quadrangle he noted with unease that it had begun to snow, a bad sign if hasty action were needed.

On the abbot's desk lay a small pile of documents.

"Have you ever seen these documents?" he asked Demara.

"Of course I have, Father. They're mine. I gave them to you," Demara said aggressively.

"This one is attested a forgery," the abbot said, holding up the confirmation certificate. "And this one. And this letter from Lawrence. And this nice note from Cardinal O'Connell is a complete fraud." He swept the papers toward Demara. "What do you have to say about this, Doctor?"

Demara was very cool. He reached for the papers and with a look of incredulous amusement began flipping through them. "Hmm. This one *is* correct. So's this. This one is all right." He looked back at the abbot. "They're all correct. They have to be. Why, they're *mine*."

Cardinal rule number one. The burden of proof is on the accuser.

Cardinal rule number two—Foch's law—then was wheeled into action. When in danger, attack!

"What can I say?" he began, slowly and sadly. "That there's been a mistake made, a serious one? But that can be corrected, Father. What can't be corrected, what can never be changed, Father," he said, his voice rising and deepening with every word, "is that you, the spiritual leader of the community, chose to doubt one of your own before even asking him whether the charge was true or not.

"You have acted like a common prosecuting attorney, not a man of God. The mistake? That is incidental. That might have happened to any man. But this hurt, this hurt in here," he patted the region around his heart, "can never be really healed. All right, you have accused me. You will find you have been wrong but you won't be able to tell me, Father. I will be gone then." He started toward the door.

"If this is the quality of your mercy and your justice, Father, then I want no part of it."

He crashed the door shut and stood out in the hall listening. It had been a splendid exit. As a man of God, of course, the abbot *would* recheck the charges to make certain no error had occurred. This would afford Demara invaluable time. He looked out the hall window. The ground was already deep in snow and he didn't relish the thought of wandering around lost in the snowy wastes of the Ozarks.

"I am good in scenes like that," Demara says, "because I *do* get outraged. There was no question in the abbot's mind that I was guilty. The ordinary faker would at least try and explain his way out at best. But I managed to plant a doubt, and once there was that doubt, for the time being at least the moral advantage was on my side. So I was outraged, of course."

He had to spoil a good part of the scene by reëntering the office, however. He opened the door and strode across the room.

"My documents," he said haughtily.

He went back to his room and packed. In Little Rock, Demara had acquired an enormous, old-fashioned, bright green steamer trunk. He had stopped to admire it in the window of a second-hand store because it was entirely plastered with stickers, good ones, from all the great hotels and resorts of the world. He realized that the green trunk would make a splendid addition to his equipage, almost as good as a second set of credentials. It would also help explain just what the doctor had been doing the preceding several years.

It was dark when he was finished packing and when he went across the schoolyard to the darkened office of the abbot the snow was well above his ankles.

It was fortunate, he thought, that he had had the foresight to have a duplicate made of the abbot's office key a few weeks before.

Inside, using a small shielded flashlight, he wrote and sent wires to over twenty-five small colleges offering them the use of his services. Some of them were bound to give an affirmative reply before letters came back from Boston verifying the fact that he was a fraud. It was quite late at night when he started back to his room, passing the school garage. He was irresistibly drawn to it and, inside, as he suspected, some trusting religious had left keys to one of the school's cars. That, of course, altered the picture since Demara was never unaware of the fact that he might be arrested for forgery before he ever got word from a college to come ahead.

In his room he shouldered the green trunk and began tiptoeing, as best as one can tiptoe with a huge trunk on one's back, down the hall and down the stairs and out to the garage. Softly he started the car's engine, the motor sounds muffled by the deep snow, and slid out into the snow. He went ten feet when the wheels began to spin helplessly. Quietly, softly, he tried to jockey the car back and forth but the tires wouldn't hold.

This is ridiculous, he thought, and he felt the taste of rage rising in his mouth. Faster and faster he began pressing down on the gas so that finally the wheels of the car were spinning furiously against the snow and brick, making a whining noise like the sound of a buzzsaw gone wild. Around him little patches of yellow began to flood out onto the snow as one after another monks and students woke up. It was as if someone were lighting a gigantic Christmas tree. Across from him he saw a light flash and then darkness and he knew someone had opened a door and was coming toward him. Presently he could see the outline of a hooded monk padding across the fuzzy whiteness in his direction.

He was trapped. Well, to hell with it, he thought. They still had nothing on him. He turned off the ignition key and the wheels slowed down in their spinning, and as they did so, the car, suddenly and rather strangely, began to crawl forward in the snow. Quickly he turned the key back on, got the engine running and found he was moving and picking up momentum. He could see that the monk was now directly in his way. He switched on his lights, there was no more need to hide, and blew his horn.

"I can't stop this thing," he shouted out the car window and just when he feared he had hit the man the monk leaped out of the way, and Demara was on his way to the highway and Fort Smith beyond. Fort Smith was the place, a soldier's town where strangers weren't closely studied.

The main road, Highway 22, had been plowed recently but only one lane was open. Whether the plow was coming his way or going the other he didn't know. What he also didn't know was that he was driving head-on into the heaviest snowfall in Arkansas in thirty years.

He didn't want to drive fast but he couldn't stop himself

from driving ahead. One of the morbid fears of his life, a residue of having seen the movie "I Was a Fugitive from a Chain Gang," was to someday wind up in a southern prison in which, he was convinced, because of his lack of discipline, he would die. The single lane actually saved him. As the car rocked from side to side and skidded from one side of the road to the other the snow banks acted as bumpers and threw him back into the right track. He drove through Paris and Caulksville and through Ratcliffe and not a person seemed to be alive in that part of Arkansas. The more distance he put between himself and New Subiaco to just that degree did he begin to relax and even begin to enjoy this wild ride through the snowy night. But when he entered the hamlet of Charleston, there was a car partially blocking the road, blinking its lights at him to stop. He began to slow down when, he insists, completely against his conscious will he felt the car pick up speed again. He knew he was going to make a run for it. He went speeding up toward the parked car in which the driver never moved, and at the very last second Demara swung his wheel to the left. He jammed the nose of the car into a snowbank, somehow got in and then out of it, and back on the road again.

It was fantastic and he was fully conscious of that. "I seemed to be able to see myself, sitting in the car, hurtling along through the darkness, never knowing when some car would be coming down the track straight for me, and all the time wondering if it was really me doing this crazy thing like something out of a movie or something some crazy, neurotic kid was always doing."

He had never driven the way he was just then and then he felt something that completely drained him of courage. In the rear of his car he felt a steady, strong bump, bump, bump. When he turned to see what it was he could not really believe his eyes.

"Here I was, risking my life every second that I drove,

doing something that only a lunatic would dare to do, and there behind me, trying to bump or edge me off the road up into the snow piles, was this hillbilly cop riding my fender. That wasn't fair. I was mad but he was far madder."

He decided to call it quits. He stepped on the brake and realized that at the speed he was traveling that was a desperate error. The car spun to one side and then seemed to begin gliding up into the air at a terrific, slipping speed. After that, trees and posts came flying toward him and he remembers praying out loud until there finally was a series of jolting thumps and tearing sounds and the car came to a stop upside down. He remembered to turn off the ignition and then, with a start, he remembered the new, shining Smith and Wesson .38 police special he had bought a few weeks before in Fort Smith. Although he could barely move, he managed to open the window enough to drop it into the snow outside before the policeman, a simple man in overalls wearing a plain, tin badge got to him.

"If you're goin' to do a thing like that, Doctor," he said softly, saddened with the idiocy of the world, "you best learn to drive right first. Now git on out."

In the police car Demara remembered his green trunk. "You just wait here," the man said and went back to the monastery car for it.

"He left the keys in the car but he knew I wouldn't run. I was licked. I've never seen a calmer, more courageous man. Many times I've tried to pattern myself after that man but I don't think I've succeeded very well."

The monastery did not want to press charges, feeling they had been sufficiently embarrassed by Demara's merely having been there. He was driven to the town of Dardanelle, where he was dumped at a bus stop with the understanding that Arkansas would see the last of him ere the sun sank on Ozark hills that night.

He wasn't unhappy. Considering where he might have

been he was in reasonably good shape. The good impostor, like the good soldier, is never caught short. His resources are hoarded and controlled to tide him over the rough spots.

There was Demara, down, disgraced but very far from out. He was on a public bus with a paid-for ticket. He had over $100 in cash he had taken from the abbey's safe in payment for four months' teaching, a move he strongly defends as being honest and proper. His green trunk was lashed to the roof of the bus and he was snug in a new, warm overcoat he found on a coat rack at Subiaco. So exuberant did he feel that when the bus passed the spot where his car had flipped the night before, he asked the driver to stop. The passengers were surprised to see the serious-looking man in the dark clerical garb begin scuffing about in the snow in the middle of the Ozark wastes. He evidently found what he was looking for, however, since they saw him stoop down and then stuff something shiny and metallic in his pocket.

Good soldier Demara was armed again. Best of all, he still had his papers. A shadow now hovered over Dr. French in Arkansas but forty-seven states still remained to be exposed to him. A good many of them would see him before he lay dead and buried.

From Arkansas he went to Kansas City, where, an hour after getting off the bus, he offered himself to the city university under the stipulation that they allow him to head up a department of psychology. He gave them the afternoon to think it over.

"Any school that needed more time than that to hire a man with my record," Demara says, "I figured to be going no place." They said that they would like to think it over a little longer, and Demara marched down to the city library in a huff and began searching through the Official Catholic Directory. He found what he felt to be the ideal place for his talents.

There was, in Chicago, an order of intellectuals called the

Clerics of St. Viator whose function was to supply Catholic communities with intellectual specialists. Demara saw a chance through them to practice his trade of psychologist and become a priest at the same time.

His two drawbacks were that he was almost broke and that his church record as Dr. French was not very savory. He would have to become a convert all over again.

In Chicago he went directly out to the provincial house of the Viatorians and had an interview with the provincial, a priest whose name was Father Richard French, which Demara took to be a happy coincidence. A less happy omen was that, although the two men reacted to each other favorably at once, Demara would not be allowed inside the provincial house until he had been converted. It would not do to admit that Dr. French, the eminent psychologist, was broke, so Demara went back downtown to see a Father William West and begin taking lessons in basic Catholic dogma.

"It was the worst time of my life. It was horrible. To get out of the cold I went to some twenty-cent movie and then I'd stay in there eighteen hours a day without any food. I shaved in bus stations and public johns and I spent hours looking in restaurant windows. Each night I had one hour of instruction and I begged the priest for more."

Even the experienced priest had to admit that Dr. French was a prodigiously fast learner. After five days he was allowed to be baptized.

"It came just in time. They didn't realize it but if one more day had gone by they would have been giving me extreme unction instead of baptizing me. It does raise a theological point. If I had starved to death as Dr. French before they baptized me, do you think my old baptism as Fred Demara would have gotten me to heaven?"

An exception to the rule of also needing to be confirmed was made in French's case and the doctor was invited to go out to the provincial house. With his last bit of money, and his absolutely last bit of strength, Demara managed to

drag his green trunk out to the Viatorians on a series of
buses. He had eleven cents when he arrived.

From the very beginning he was a success with the Viatorians, and in Father French he found a man he could admire. His first serious challenge came when it was announced
that, despite his degrees, so that he could acquire a solid
Catholic background, he was being entered in De Paul University for a graduate crash course in theology. De Paul is a
large university with some 6,000 students and is considered
one of the more academically demanding Catholic colleges.

Father French handed Demara his list of studies and
Demara felt a sudden sinking sensation in the region around
his heart. The list read:

> Rational Psychology
> Metaphysics
> Cosmology
> Epistemology
> Ethics
> Natural Theology

"I know that's quite an order," Father French said, "but
we figured that with your very extensive background and
brilliant record you should be able to handle this. If you
can't, why, we'll just drop one or two and you can make
them up next term. If you can, we'll save time," he added.

"I feel sure I can, Father," Demara said, with a breeziness
that could have been taken for arrogance.

"How else was I to act?" he says. "When I walked into
my first course I couldn't pronounce it properly. I couldn't
have explained the titles of two thirds of them. I was sick
with fright."

He tried hard and he studied hard and he did as was
expected of him. His grades were brilliant. Of the six
courses, the man who in real life had not quite managed

the second year of high school scored a record of straight A's.

"I knew I could do it but I had to have it proven to me. That experience really changed me. No matter how I might feel I still can't work up any respect for acquired learning. I can for character but not learning. A man with a good mind who trusts it can learn anything he needs to know in a few months."

A question that puzzles people is how Demara, with such a very limited background, avoided exposure during such things as academic and scholarly arguments and debates. His answer shows a cunning and instinctive grasp of the rules that guide human conduct.

"I wasn't afraid of that kind of exposure," he says. "The reason is simple. I always lost the debate."

It went this way. If he made a statement and it was challenged Demara would ask—"How do *you* think it should go?" As the man explained Demara would nod his head wisely and, at times, even take notes. This was high flattery indeed.

"Did they think I was feeble-minded or badly informed when I sat down and listened to them? How many arguments have *you* ever won in your life? Arguments where the person you were arguing with suddenly said 'By George, you're right. I never looked at it that way before. You've convinced me.' Would you think that person was ignorant? You would not. You'd say, Now there's a man who's willing to listen to the truth and who can recognize it when he sees it."

Because he was wise enough to flatter the pedant which lurks in the soul of every man, Demara established a reputation as a fair-minded scholar. No one apparently ever sensed the enormous holes in his academic background.

"How could they when I let them do all the talking?" he asks.

A natural blessing is that he is able to fill holes in his background quickly. He has a flair for picking up essential information. In his trade he is what is known as a quick study.

Another reason for his excellent grades might also have been that he made sure to cover every one of his papers with a note written on small, expensive, discreet stationery. At the top of the paper his name and academic titles were listed and in the upper left-hand corner, always inked out by Demara so that you could barely read it, was By Appointment Only. Assistant instructors getting papers from a practicing Ph. D. in psychology might naturally be hesistant about grading him down.

And then there was his "official" stamp, a seal such as notary publics use. It was circular, and stamped on the bottom of papers, leaving them with a large, embossed seal, it gave them a weighty, solid look. At the top of the impression was his name, at the bottom his occupation of psychologist and in the middle of the seal his motto: *ESSE QUAM VIDERE.*

That was the most splendid joke of all. Translated it means: TO BE, NOT TO SEEM TO BE.

There were several dangerous moments that year. One of them happened when Demara drove down to Union Station to meet Father French, who was returning from a trip. He was settling Father French in the car when elements of the beach battalion Demara had served with years before, who were then on their way at last to the Pacific and war, walked by him.

"Hey, aren't you . . . ?" one Marine began. Several others also thought they recognized him and crowded around the car as Father French stared with curiosity at the scene. The Marines realized they were wrong as they looked at the man's white turned-around collar and clerical clothes.

"Sorry, Father," they mumbled and went on their way, shouldering their barracks bags and turning around every once in a while to scratch their heads. It was winter but Demara could feel the cold sweat running down his body.

"Strange, isn't it? They thought they knew me in the Navy."

"Very strange," Father French said.

Since Father French was the only person Demara talked to, it was from him that he would most have to fear detection. Demara has a very thick, South Boston, Massachusetts mill-town accent. He says *pack* for park, *juuurk* for jerk and such things as *buh-day-duz* for potatoes. Occasionally he calls a truck a wagon and refers to soft drinks, such as Coca-Cola, as tonic, pronounced *twon-ic*. Amazingly he was not conscious of having any marked accent.

"Where in the world did you ever *get* that accent, Robert?" Father French once asked him.

"What accent, Father?"

"Now, Robert, don't pretend you don't know. Why, you have one of those New England accents you hear satirized on the radio. Very thick. *Very* thick, indeed."

"Well, my parents *were* from outside Boston, Father," Demara said.

"But I thought you said your people were from Michigan," Father French said, giving him a sharp and curious look.

"Oh, they grew *up* in Michigan. They were born and raised around Boston."

"Amazing to retain that accent and then pass it on to you. Didn't the children in school ridicule you?"

"No. Then we always had these serving girls from Boston. Good Irish-Catholic girls, just off the boat. We were sort of an underground railroad for getting Irish girls out west and getting husbands."

"But you told me you were poor!"

"Oh, we didn't *pay* them anything, Father. Just room and board until they found a husband, you know."

"Why are you sweating so, Robert?"

"It's hot in here, isn't it, Father?"

"On the contrary, it's cold. I was going to ask you to turn up the heat."

A person with the instincts of a policeman would have done a certain amount of puzzled pondering after a session such as the one above. It was Demara's luck that Father French had the instincts of a saint.

About his background, wherever he was later to go, Demara discovered a very vital thing for his future.

"I call it, Demara's law for passing, or, the invisible past. Almost all impostors, I have found, cut out a picture of what they think they should look like and then they begin piling up mounds of plausible sounding information behind that silhouette. Say they are supposed to come from Saginaw. What do they do? They learn the name of the high school, of some streets, all sorts of information. When someone mentions Saginaw they leap right in spouting information left and right. This, they feel, proves they *must* be genuine. But I say, once they mention anything definite, they are now on record. I never mention *anything*. Don't be too obvious about not mentioning anything but always leave them with a shadow. If you meet someone who does come from Saginaw you have got to change the conversation or let him do the talking, which, if you lead him the right way, he will do. It really works. Wherever I have left, people are always suddenly amazed to find they don't know one damn thing about me, where I was supposed to come from and have been, although they all thought they did, that is until the police began asking for specifics. That's Demara's law for seeming to be real and staying as loose and free as a wild goose."

At the end of the highly successful school year at De Paul and with the Clerics of St. Viator, Father French announced that it was time for Dr. French to begin his full novitiate training with an eye toward taking his sacred vows for the priesthood. This would take place at the now defunct St. Viator's college in central Illinois.

"But Father, I thought I could take it here," Demara protested. He was afraid of another novitiate.

"I like to think that I just couldn't bring myself to actively begin preparing for the priesthood. I mean, I was a fake, all right, but I had scruples and a sense of honor and decency. I couldn't become a priest."

Equally persuasive, however, was the factor of boredom, a thing for which Demara suffers a low threshold of tolerance. From his first day he ran afoul of the novice master and each day grew worse.

"Every time they started on the day's lesson, something I'd done eight times before, I felt this wild devil trying to get out of me, like one of those smoking genii trying to push the cork out of the bottle and escape. He usually got out. Oh, I was funny there. I was a howling wit. I think I was personally responsible for causing at least three or four novices to begin wondering if the Church was all a big joke and fraud. I was good enough to know that it was time to pack my green trunk and get."

He went back to Chicago where he had a tearful parting with Father French. His promising career in the Viatorians was over. To this day he feels humiliated by his need, as he was going out the door of the provincial house, to filch a fistful of Father French's stationery before heading on.

From Chicago he went to Milwaukee, where he joined the Order of St. Camillus. The Camillians, a heavily German group, ran a hospital where Demara felt he could use his knowledge of psychology, and they also had a scholasticate —a house of studies for philosophers and theologians— which might prove to be a good base of operations for writing the various papers Demara was still seriously considering writing

Before doing this, however, there was the necessity for learning the value of humility and for taking a basic noviatiate. This was almost too much and when he was put in the kitchen preparing German dishes, the end was not far away.

There was an old priest who didn't like or trust Demara. To the embarrassment of the community he said on seeing him, "If that man is a doctor, I'll eat my cassock."

And he didn't care for Demara's way with food.

"Oh, *you're* cooking tonight," he said one evening. "I'm glad I was warned. I'll go get my hammer and saw," he said acidly.

"I was determined to be humble if I had to bust a gut doing it," Demara says. "But that was it, the breaking point."

The plate of sauerbraten went crashing to the floor, followed by a string of oaths that rang clear and true through the dining hall for all to hear, interspersed with the crash of crockery being dropped systematically on the kitchen floor.

The last the Camillians ever saw of Dr. French was the rear view of his green trunk as he carried it out to the highway, the late rays of sunshine glittering off the hundred multi-hued stickers like flecks of rain sparkling on a peacock's tail.

Back in Chicago he borrowed money from Father French and headed toward New York, feeling that the anonymity of the great city offered him the best chance to begin a new life. While on the way, riding a bus through Indiana, it was announced that the war with Japan was over. The bus turned into an island of wild, exuberant people rocking through the darkness of the night, until they sang and drank themselves into a delirious coma. In the morning he was the first to wake up, and as he surveyed the scene of wreckage around him, he found himself staring at his reflection in the window as if he could see through himself. He took stock of his life.

He was twenty-four years old and in robust health. He had a peculiar duplicity of features that enabled him to look at

one moment like a knowledgeable cherub and at the next as
a stern, serious-minded man. His worst physical drawback
was a tendency to gain weight but as long as he stayed in the
religious world that could be controlled. He weighed about
235 pounds but his enormous frame could carry that weight
easily. Pictures of him then show that he looks much like any
lineman on a professional football team.

"I was in wonderful shape," he says. "I had developed a
beautiful set of muscles lugging that damn green trunk
around."

Spiritually the picture was not as healthy. He had been
in an even dozen Catholic orders or organizations and had
been asked to leave every one of them, which, even at that
stage of his career he suspected was a new low for an American Catholic.

No matter how he looked at it, he was forced to admit he
had been a religious reprobate. The only way to correct that,
he felt, was to reënter the religious life and this time succeed
at it. What was needed was exactly the right place for a man
of his talents and he determined this time to find that spot.

To tide himself over in New York while finding the right
place he went to the Paulist fathers, accompanied by a letter
from his "uncle," Father Richard French, and was sent out
to the Paulist novitiate in Oak Ridge, New Jersey, in the
mountains of New Jersey. There he began a campaign of
sending out feelers to small Catholic colleges where he felt
he could do his best work. His one worry was that a letter
of testimony about him from Chicago would reach Oak
Ridge before he was ready to leave. That fear was greatly
relieved when he found that by simply volunteering to go
down to the highway for the mail he could, as it were, control and censor the incoming mail. That took a lot of pressure
off the young novice. When the letter from the Chicago archdiocese did come, it was quite simple for Demara to inter-
cept it and open it.

Things were worse than he had thought. His record was in seemy shape. Demara pocketed the letter.

A week or so later he finally heard from a new, fast-growing Catholic college in Erie, Pennsylvania, named Gannon. They would be delighted they informed him to have a conference about setting up a department of psychology at Gannon with Dr. French in charge.

That was what he had been waiting for. In the privacy of his cubicle he got out the green trunk and packed it and that night he carried it out to the highway. At the mailbox he made sure to enclose the letter of testimony from Chicago. He wanted to go out clean as a whistle with a fresh slate waiting to be crammed with good and even glorious deeds. He knew he had done several things purists might term bad in applying to Gannon, but to him evil of this sort, since the end result is for the good, is merely evil in the abstract. If good occurs, evil never happened.

Everything was fine. It was early autumn in 1945, he would be ready for the start of the new school year, and he was certain he had found his place in life.

12

The interview was an unqualified success. Monsignor Joseph Wehrle, who had been fearful of meeting some stiff, pompous windbag, was pleasantly surprised to be faced with an exuberant, obviously willing and energetic young man. Demara felt similarly toward Reverend Wehrle. What had begun as a stiff, bargaining session soon was fizzing and bubbling merrily.

"I want to be frank with you, Doctor. What would bring a man with your credentials to a place like Gannon?" he was asked.

"And I want to be frank with you, Father. I want to become a good Catholic convert but I also want to be able to grow with a school and leave my mark on it forever."

Most of what he said was true. Demara has always had a strong urge to be the founder of something and to have his name put on a building or plaque, possibly as some tangible evidence of his existence. This sort of feeling was understandable to Monsignor Wehrle. At the end of their meeting both men felt themselves to be old and fast friends.

"I want you to stay right here with me," Wehrle said with sudden enthusiasm. "There is a large, extra room right down the hall on the second floor of the manor house and I wish you would consider taking it."

It was agreed to. As Dr. French left to get his green trunk at the station he paused in the doorway.

"Oh, one other little thing," he said smoothly. "About my title."

"Oh, yes," Wehrle said and sat down. Both men thought for some several minutes. "Well, you can't be president because I'm president," he finally said. "How about Chairman of the Department of Psychology?"

A disappointed look crossed Demara's face and they thought again. It was a fine and delicate point.

"Considering the vast, inevitable growth of Gannon," Demara finally said softly, "wouldn't Dean of the School of Philosophy be more in keeping?"

He saw the monsignor stiffen slightly. It was a little much, Demara thought, but it was worth the trying. He had pushed him hard but at last he saw him relax. "All right, I'm sold," the Right Reverend Wehrle said, rising to his feet and holding out his hand. "*Dean* of the *School* of Philosophy it is."

"If anyone at Gannon had been fortunate enough to have been in just the right place then they could have seen their new dean doing such a prance and such a caper that it is certain that no other dean of any other school of philosophy has ever or will ever match it.

He went downtown to retrieve his trunk but before he ever got to the station he stopped at the first top quality printing establishment he passed. He ordered several hundred calling cards and a few dozen boxes of stationery and had them engraved.

Doctor Robert Linton French, B.S., M.S., PH.D. *Psychology*
       Dean of the School of Philosophy
              Gannon University

                                    BY APPOINTMENT ONLY

Gannon was only a college but Demara had plans for its growth. The green trunk was carried upstairs and placed in the doctor's room.

Dr. French plunged into work with an enthusiasm rarely seen around a college outside of the football squad. No chore was too small for the eager doctor and he was willing to take on anything. A standard routine, soon to become a campus tradition, was for Demara to race into a class, peer at his watch, peer at his students, and ask, "What am I teaching?"

By mid-year the dean had blocked out and was teaching courses in general psychology, industrial psychology and abnormal psychology. It should be said that during the years Demara had been passing as Dr. French he had been doing a haphazard but massive amount of reading, and he had collected an undigested, uncollated but remarkable amount of psychological information.

On all of this Demara bloomed. He had always been a good talker and given his awesome title he became a self-assured spellbinder. One of his favorite topics, delivered at Rotarian meetings, American Legion conclaves and the like was "Growing Gannon and Its Role in Erie." It is said that he made this subject positively exciting.

He let it be known that he was the reformed black sheep of a very wealthy Protestant family and heir to real money. This, he found, made him attractive to all kinds of people. He was such a popular speaker at women's clubs that he was finally persuaded to write a booklet embodying his philosophy. He did. It is titled "How To Bring Up Your Child," and the core of its thinking is to shower the child with love and quit worrying about spoiling it. Copies are still around Erie.

Monsignor Wehrle was delighted with his "catch," but as the months rolled by, little things, and then bigger ones, rose to cause him worry and instill the ugly shadow of doubt in his mind. He began to sense that instead of a brilliant lamb in the fold he was holding on to a tiger by the tail. The major complaint, as always, was that Demara went ahead on all kinds of grandiose projects and asked permission later.

One of the simplest areas of abrasion lay in that Wehrle possessed a large, fierce but lovable Norwegian elkhound who for some reason detested Dr. French. Whenever the good doctor passed in the hall or came anywhere near the dog, the beast curled back his lip, snarled and foamed at the mouth and did its level best to get a chunk of the dean. In turn, whenever the dean had a quiet chance he proceeded to let the dog know that he, Dr. French, cared as little for it as it did for him.

"Either that dog goes or I go," French said one night, and when he saw by the look on Wehrle's face that the dog certainly wasn't going to be the first to go, he was deeply hurt and resentful.

And there was the famous beer incident. So highly keyed up by his work that he found it hard to sleep, Demara began going out and buying a half a dozen or a dozen bottles of beer at night to induce drowsiness. These he bought each evening in a nearby tavern and brought back to his room in a small laundry hamper. One night Wehrle stepped out of his room into the hall just as the doctor was returning.

"Well, getting your laundry *again*, eh, Doctor?" he asked.

"Cleanliness is next to godliness," the doctor replied, chuckling, whereupon the monsignor gave the hamper a fairly hard boot with his foot. The tinkle of breaking glass and after that the rich smell of beer soon flooded the hallway. A trickle became a stream and the beer flowed along the edge of the hall until it reached the staircase, where it became a foaming waterfall.

"Oh, you've broken my bottle of beer," Demara said. Wehrle eyed the hissing, frothing flood pouring down his balustrade.

"Bottle!" he said. "Bottle!"

"Yes. And I'll have to charge you two cents for the deposit," Demara said.

All of these incidents, and there were many like them, were especially unfortunate since for several months Demara had been acquiring a following and rounding up support for his greatest project. His dream was to establish a "society of pious laymen for the instruction of Catholic youth," using Gannon as a home base or provincial house. The idea was patterned after the Clerics of St. Viator.

"My theory was—if you can't join 'em, beat 'em," Demara says.

He had done his original spadework well. He had already gotten the approbation of Erie's bishop, John Mark Gannon, who had generously offered the use of a house near the college as the order's first home. The "order" was to be called—The Pious Society of St. Mark.

Although much remained to be done Demara had already placed an ad in several national Catholic weeklies advertising for men who were willing to pioneer and be trail blazers—men who wanted to be founders and "get in on the ground floor of a great new educational adventure."

"I figured that would draw the usual number of phonies, crackpots and genuine talent. I didn't care about the quality too much at first just so I had quantity."

So as not to "bother" anyone at Gannon, Demara rented a post office box to handle the flood of applicants.

Applicants were advised to reply to Brother Robert Copernicus.

"I wasn't a religious then, of course, but I had fresh *literas*. As soon as I had a big enough bunch I expected to get official church recognition through Bishop Gannon and go right into the Church at the top of an order of brothers."

It was during all this activity that a thing happened which was to profoundly change Demara's attitude at Gannon. The school had taken on as instructor a priest with bad lung trouble who could not climb stairs. Because of this Wehrle reluctantly asked Dr. French to give up his large room on the second floor and move upstairs into a smaller, darker room.

"It was like being shoved into the attic. I felt I had been exiled to Siberia. It was silly of me but I couldn't get it out of my head that I was being punished. I also felt I lost one hell of a lot of prestige. Students used to like to come to my room for a chat and conference but I was ashamed to bring them up to the garret."

He determined to resolve that situation. One afternoon Wehrle, at work in his office, was surprised to see a group of men struggle past his door and upstairs with what appeared to be a rug. Soon after that he heard pounding noises and later another group of men grunted by with a large crate. When the pounding continued into early evening he went up to investigate. The third floor had never looked like that before.

The hall was carpeted and above French's door was a sign announcing his office. Inside the room was carpeted prettily from wall to wall. On top of the rug was a great, gleaming, blond maple desk. Behind the desk was Demara.

"Delighted you could drop by," Demara said. "Now you can answer this. Should the desk stay where it is or should I put it by the window?"

Wehrle was taken aback. He was no student of modern furniture but he could see that the cost of the things around him was high. But then he recalled the rumors of French's wealth and assumed that was the source of the money. "I would leave it where it is," he said cheerfully and went back downstairs. In the ensuing days a typewriter, a couch, new drapes and, finally, an enormous cherrywood bed were delivered.

At last the school of philosophy had an office worthy of its dean. As far as Gannon and the dean were concerned, Dr. French had arrived.

But so had the bills. A stack of them. All made out to

Gannon in Monsignor Wehrle's name. Clutching a ream of the first ones that arrived, the monsignor ran through the halls until he found French leaning against a blackboard, passing pleasantries with the student body.

"Come out," he said in a strange way, fluttering the bills in his hand as though he held a wild bird by the wing.

"EXPLAIN!" he finally choked out.

"Why, Father," Demara said softly in a voice as pulpy as an eggplant, "what's to explain? You saw me getting those things and never said a word. If I did something wrong then you-led-me-on."

It is fortunate for Demara that Monsignor Wehrle was a Christian gentleman and that he also didn't happen to be holding a club in his hand. There is some possibility that even this debacle might have been overlooked if it hadn't been for the safe.

It was a large gray, double-doored steel chest, much bigger than the one the university owned. Some workmen were in the process of wedging it upstairs in the manner of the pyramid builders when Wehrle returned.

"Save your energy," he ordered the men. "This is going back."

"It can't go back, Father," Demara said. "I got it on sale before you told me I couldn't sign any more Gannon purchase orders."

Wehrle was very obviously having a struggle to control himself. "What do you need it for?" he asked in a trembly voice.

"Why, my personal records," Dr. French said. "I think someone has been searching my room."

"And just who do you think has been searching your room?"

Shamelessly Demara stood, in full view of the workmen, and eyed the monsignor. "Oh, if I could only have that cold stare back!" he has since said.

"It could be *anyone*," Demara said, and he went upstairs.

Several hours later there was a knock on his door and the monsignor appeared. "I'm sorry about what happened. It's been a hard several months and we're tired and edgy. But I think you'll agree that I had good cause."

"Yes, I'll agree," Demara said. They sat in silence, neither man knowing how to back down gracefully.

"What's come between us?" Demara finally said and at the same moment Wehrle said, "Why is it that we can't seem to understand each other better?"

They both laughed then and for a while they talked as they had in the early days. At last Wehrle got up to go back downstairs.

"So you'll ask them to come and get the safe tomorrow anyway, then?" Wehrle said.

"Is that an ultimatum?" Demara snapped, and the moment the words had gotten loose from between his teeth, he wanted them back. They were so cold and swift and so hard.

"But I didn't know how to back down from them. I didn't want to lose face and prestige. I looked around my proud, grand office and I knew I could never take those words back."

"If you want to make it an ultimatum," Wehrle said, "then I will be forced to make it one."

"What you're asking for is my dismissal then, isn't it?" Demara said.

"What is wrong with you?"

"That's what you want, isn't it?"

There was no answer. The monsignor started for the door. "When you are prepared to come upstairs and withdraw your ultimatum, I will be waiting for you. Meanwhile, I'll be packing."

His idea, he now thinks, was to force the situation to such an exaggerated point that it would be silly for one side not to back down. And at one step backward by the other man he could feel he had been victorious.

"Don't ask me why I had to win that battle. I was Dean of the School of Philosophy and I had to have all my respect. Oh, I was very proud."

He began packing the green trunk slowly, waiting for the sound of a door opening downstairs and the sound of footsteps on the stairs. For hours he packed until he could stall no longer, and as he was finishing he began to realize the enormity of his mistake. He loved it there and in his combative way he loved Wehrle and now he didn't want to leave but he didn't know how to stop.

"Why won't you come to save me from myself?" he wanted to shout down the stairwell but he didn't. Instead he began dragging the big trunk along the hall and down the steps. He moved slowly, one thump down at a time and a short wait, giving Wehrle a chance to stop him. On the second floor he passed the monsignor's darkened office. Outside the door rested the gray safe, and with surprise Demara realized that he was crying. Great, soft tears were quietly rolling down his cheeks. He hurried then so that the monsignor wouldn't see that he was crying. Downstairs in the foyer he skidded the trunk across the floor. As he did so a flood of yellow spread out into the hall above, and Demara could make out the form of the monsignor in the doorway.

"You're too late, Wehrle," Demara called out. "I waited too long." He picked up the trunk and hefted it onto his shoulder.

"I only wanted to say, God go with you, Robert," Wehrle's voice came softly and sadly down the staircase.

"He'd better stay here, Father. You need Him more than I do."

Bitterness was too cheap a luxury for the occasion but he couldn't think of anything magnanimous or memorable to say. In fact his very last words at Gannon were "Ah, nuts," as the green trunk momentarily jammed in the doorway and had to be wriggled loose.

He went out into the soft spring night, the trunk bobbing on his back, feeling as low and mean and miserable as he ever had before in his life.

13

THE END OF THE TRUNK

From Erie he took a train westward. Railroads have a policy of allowing members of religious groups half-fare who can show small identifying courtesy cards. Demara had made sure to get one. He was traveling as Brother Robert Copernicus. His religious order: The Pious Society of St. Mark.

"So Gannon wasn't a complete loss. I still have the card and I still use it," Demara says.

When he reached Chicago, he decided he needed time to plan and entered as a postulant the Abbey of St. Bede, a Benedictine house in Peru, Illinois, where he sorely tried their patience.

"It was a stopover, a free hotel until I got my bearings."

It was to prove to be one of the most costly free hotels in his history.

He found an order in California that looked promising and he headed for Los Angeles, only stopping along the way to visit Bishop Duane G. Hunt of Salt Lake City, where he lifted a handful of the bishop's invaluable green stationery. In Los Angeles he became "converted" again, to give Dr. French yet another fresh letter of testimony, and joined the Brothers of St. John of God, a small group of men who ran a hospital. He determined to make a sensational impression.

After "papering" himself with letters from Bishop Hunt he rented a chauffeur-driven limousine and had himself carried out West Adams Boulevard to the brothers' hospital.

"Poor chap," he said of the driver as he left him, "I'll have to let him go. Been with me for years."

After all this, he was dealt a major blow, however, one from which he couldn't recover: the hospital was actually a home for the aged.

"What could they do with a psychologist? The best advice I had in most cases was euthenasia, but then that wouldn't go over well with the outfit I was in—if you get what I mean. The company director in Rome would be sure to object."

He began searching again through the Catholic Directory. The heat of summer made his mind turn increasingly to the cool greens of the Pacific Northwest and he finally found the ideal place for him. It was St. Martin's Abbey and College, a small, fifty-year-old abbey and college run by the Benedictines in Olympia, Washington, just outside of Seattle.

As he left, one of the more embarrassing incidents in his career happened. On the way out to the hospital he had stopped to buy two doctor's jackets and he had since then worn them daily. Just as he was going, a young brother said, "I've always wanted to ask you, Doctor. Why do you prefer those jackets you wear?"

"Those jackets? What about my jackets? What's wrong with them?"

"I didn't mean anything by the question. I just wanted to know what advantage you felt you got out of wearing barber's jackets."

For the first time in many years Demara found himself blushing. The erstwhile doctor slunk out of the hospital dragging his trunk behind him.

He determined, for the first time in his life, to make a careful, plotted, scientific assault on St. Martin's. He had now had a wide range of experience behind him, and it was time, he felt, to begin to use what he had learned about institutions and people and how they function.

He had come to two beliefs. One was that in any organization there is always a lot of loose, unused power lying about which can be picked up without alienating anyone.

The second rule is, if you want power and want to expand, never encroach on anyone else's domain; open up new ones.

"I call it 'Expanding into the power vacuum,'" Demara proudly explains. "It works this way. If you come into a new situation (there's a nice word for it) don't join some other professor's committee and try to make your mark by moving up in that committee. You'll, one, have a long haul and two, make an enemy."

Demara's technique is to found your own committee.

"That way there's no competition, no past standards to measure you by. How can anyone tell you aren't running a top outfit? And then there's no past laws or rules or precedents to hold you down or limit you. Make your own rules and interpretations. Nothing like it. Remember it—expand into the power vacuum!"

With these principles in mind, Demara descended on unsuspecting St. Martin's. He felt the place to be ideal for him at once and the people there took to Demara at once. He didn't expand, however. Exploded is closer to it. The Benedictines, whose motto is, To Work Is to Pray, divide themselves between spiritual, intellectual and physical work. Dr. French leaped into all three pursuits. He amazed the community with his eagerness to learn Church dogma and his ability to do it (by this time he had it pretty well memorized) and with his physical strength. He is, as we have said, a most powerful man. And the intellectuals of the community were not allowed to miss the fact that Dr. French had amassed a powerful academic background. To his regular marks, he could not resist adding his real grades at De Paul, not so much from greed as from a hope that they might just get him out of serving another novitiate. This was to prove to be a serious error. He also let it slip out shortly after his arrival that he was also a doctor of medicine. Members of the abbey began coming to him for medical treatment.

Demara's justification for allowing this is refreshingly simple.

"The seriously sick know they're sick and so do you. Those you send to a hospital. The rest are all going to get better sooner or later, and anything you do for them will seem right, and because they think you're a doctor, they'll automatically feel better."

One night, however, an old monk staggered into his cubicle suffering from a heart attack. Terrified, realizing the man was dying, Demara shouted for help and an ambulance. The doctor who finally arrived could not understand how Dr. French had failed to take even the most basic, elementary steps to help the monk. This puzzled others as well; for one, the Right Reverend Raphael Heider, the abbot of St. Martin's. But the incident was soon forgotten.

At the beginning of the school year Demara struck hard into the power vacuum. Without waiting for approval, he commandeered a school room, had it repainted and decorated and organized The St. Martin's Student Psychological Center. The center offered a series of introductory lectures by Dr. French on basic psychology and also offered private psychological sessions for students needing help. As a regular teacher he was on probation until they could examine his work but the psychological center was booming. No one seemed to know exactly how to curb his enthusiasms and since he wasn't invading any sacred domains no one objected.

He also expanded out into public life. He noted that his fellow monks had little touch with the outside, and he felt it would be a solid position to be go-between with the monastery and the town. His technique was masterfully simple. He went each afternoon to some different government office and announced his presence.

"Hello, there," he would boom out. "I am Dr. Robert French—er, excuse me, I *was* Dr. French. I am now Brother Robert French of St. Martin's. I'm new out here in your wonderful West and I thought I had better learn how you handle things out here. By the looks of things, I'd say you are handling them wonderfully."

Within weeks he could list among his "friends" many of the highest ranking members of the Olympia official family. Few politicians could resist the cheerful monk. He became especially close to Sheriff Frank Tamblyn, who was soon to be running for reëlection and saw in Demara a nice link with both the Catholic and the egg-head vote.

During this time Abbot Heider had gone East to attend an educational conference, and it was while he was there that he heard some disquieting things. He mentioned the doctor who had "dropped out of the blue" to, as fate would have it, the abbot of St. Bede's, where Demara had spent a few weeks. He was warned that this Dr. French, since it must be the same man, was considered a very bad actor. Heider determined to put Dr. French under close watch.

By the time he returned to Washington he found that Demara had accomplished the rather incredible feat of getting himself appointed an honorary deputy sheriff with the right to carry a gun and have a siren and searchlight on his car. He had become a notary public. He had been appointed an honorary official in the fire department with certain real and special privileges. And his application to become a justice of the peace was pending. For a man who wasn't even a registered voter, the jolly Benedictine was breaking political speed records.

By use of an old vaudeville routine Demara had also managed to persuade everyone at St. Martin's that he was rich. He joined two banks, and at least once a day he was to be seen by some member of the community depositing or taking out of one of the banks a "roll that would choke a horse." The roll was mostly green paper and singles but it looked like much more.

"Always try to appear rich," Demara says. "It automatically confers respect and consideration on a person. The only times I've been treated really badly was when people *knew* I wasn't rich. There is a mysterious awe toward money that rubs off on the guy who has it, don't kid yourself."

He stuck to his rules of conduct except in one thing. He invaded the realm of the football coach. For years Demara had entertained the theory that football should be purely fun. The team that had most fun would win in the end because they would bring more zest to the game. The second part of the theory was that one should adopt the principles of Gandhi. If someone knocked you down you should smile charmingly at him. If you blocked somebody out, you came back and helped the man up.

"It was a policy of massive, passive resistance. The other team would soon lose all desire to hit you since the first concern of all Americans is to be liked."

Dr. French went about inculcating these ideas into some of the players, to the complete dismay of the coach. In front of his eyes the intruder was changing St. Martin's tigers into kittens whose prospects of beating such teams at Runkle Rural High were not bright. He protested vehemently to Abbot Heider.

The abbot of St. Bede's had mentioned that Dr. French had let slip the fact that he had once been at New Subiaco, and one afternoon, after a monk had reported to him that he had watched Dr. French consume a full quart of whiskey the night before without so much as batting an eye, Abbot Heider sent out a probing letter to both De Paul and New Subiaco.

"That whiskey thing was a real mistake. Among the lesser monks I let it be known that I was really an alcoholic putting up a terrific battle against the bottle. I've observed that alcoholics get praise heaped on them just for not drinking. I was trying to arrange it so that I would get a medal every day for not being drunk. Who knows. If I had stayed off altogether and managed to exaggerate the depths of my degradation over the years, they might have made me a saint. I can see it—Sanctus Demarius, patron saint of the Bowery."

Even before the letter came back from New Subiaco, Abbot Heider's suspicions that something was not right with French were heightened by another incident. Since the college was expanding, the abbot felt it would be a good idea to get out a new brochure about the school and, especially, its staff. When French heard about the project he asked to be put in charge. He did a good job on the brochure with one exception. When the proofs were returned there was no mention or picture of Dr. French.

"I don't go in for that kind of publicity," he said grandly. "It's all right for the others to glorify themselves but for a doctor of my stature it is considered unethical and demeaning. My works will speak for themselves," he added.

Then the letter from New Subiaco arrived with all kinds of corroborating evidence. Demara was sitting in his cubicle, preparing a one-minute recorded campaign speech for Sheriff Tamblyn (one was already being played all over Thurston County) when a monk appeared and said that the abbot would like to see him.

Demara was highly pleased. He had asked the busy abbot to put aside some time that day so that he could discuss his plan for starting a fund-raising campaign to build a small new building that would house the (French) psychological center.

When he got to the abbot's office he wasn't surprised to see Sheriff Tamblyn there since the two men had become close friends. The presence of the other two strangers, however, did puzzle him.

"Good to see you, Frank," he said heartily. "Got the speech all shipshape and ready to go."

"Good to see *you*, Ferdinand," one of the strangers said.

There was no reaction evident on Demara's face. He simply stood stunned and blank. He watched one of the men open and close a wallet, and he realized that this was federal business. The FBI. Probably criminal business. He had just enough control of himself to say nothing. The first thing was to see what they wanted.

"So it *is* true, Robert," Abbot Heider sadly said.

"What's true?" Demara said bitterly. "That I tried to do a good job here to make up for a bad background? That I tried my very best?"

One of the agents held a pair of handcuffs in his hands. "I don't need those," he said angrily, and they were put away.

"Now is the best time to take him," Heider said. "The rest are at lunch."

They took him out to the car where he began regaining control of himself.

"Good God," he said. "I almost forgot. The green trunk."

They let him go back and pack and when he came back, there was a knot of students waiting. Word had gotten around.

"I feel I should have something to say to them," Demara said to one agent, "but for the life of me all I can think of is, Have fun, you're only young once. That's not exactly the sort of thing they put on statues, is it?"

He wasn't embarrassed by the students' stares since he felt clear and clean. He had done no harm there. He even, he had to admit, rather enjoyed being the center of attention. In the car they settled comfortably and rolled out toward the main gate of the school.

"I'm sorry to leave here. It was a fine place," he said. "Now, where to?"

"Why, the Navy detention barracks in Seattle," an agent said in surprise. "Why, was there anything else?"

He leaped in surprise. For some reason he had completely forgotten the military charges, perhaps because, of all the things against him, they were the worst.

"Desertion!" one said.

"In time of war," the second added.

"The penalty is death," the first said sadly.

They left him at the barracks where he was booked and placed in a cell. Through the bars he could see his beloved trunk sitting out in a passageway. "Hey, what about my trunk?" he asked. He saw two slim young prisoners lift it to their shoulders and totter away with it. Against the deep green, especially under the naked light bulbs and against the drabness of the walls, the stickers looked gay and cheerful.

"I thought then that I only wished I had the money I'd spent on glue to keep those stickers on. I did like that trunk."

"Buddy, you have *really* been around," a guard said admiringly.

"And like the bad penny, I've always turned up. Tell them to take care of that trunk, please," Demara said.

But they didn't. That was the last he ever saw of the green trunk.

The charge, as the FBI agents rightly said, *was* desertion in time of war, and the penalty *was* death.

"It was much too important to be left in the hands of lawyers. I felt I was familiar with all those little twists and veerings in my career that would only baffle a Navy lawyer. What I needed was a kind of honest liar. I was the exact man for the job."

They gave him a copy of the judge advocate's file, a copy of the Navy Code and a booklet which proved to be a cram course in instant legal defense. After a week of study he found his plea: Guilty with mitigating circumstances.

He was wise enough to know that his case needed a good deal of showmanship and not too much legal knowledge. Of course the charge was still one that called for the death penalty. Even the aged court clerk groaned when the seaman said he was going to handle his own case.

He had a month to prepare his case but he couldn't study for it. There was nothing to study. His plan was to throw himself on the mercy of the court and leave his soul in their, and God's, hands.

On the morning of his trial they fitted him out with a uniform so small that it didn't come close to fitting and he was pleased. He looked more simple and in need of guidance than he had since he was a child of five.

There is today no full record extant of what took place in that court-martial and that is society's loss and a literary shame. From every report, Demosthenes would have been hard put to have held his own against the boy orator of Lawrence.

After the formal charge and the dull, prosaic questions on which the law insists, he began his defense. He told them how, as a young lad just fresh out of a Trappist monastery, on an impulse of pure and idealistic patriotism, he joined the Navy. There, instead of finding the idealistic men he had hoped to meet, he fell into the company of hardened, salty, foul-talking seamen.

He explained to them how at first he had been stunned and shamed, and then shocked, sickened and demoralized.

With a trace of tears and a struggling hoarseness growing in his throat he told how he had finally fraudulently tried to become an officer and a gentleman in the vain hope that he might avoid the sordid, corrupt and degrading role that was straining the limits of his soul.

Failing at that, in the end he had run to the sheltering arms of Gethsemani, where he belonged. As he explained the place to them, every officer must have felt more worldly and blacker than the man he was trying.

Fred Demara was found guilty with mitigating circumstances. From a tough court-martial, he got a sentence of six years, one for each year of desertion.

When word of the sentence spread through the prison it created a sensation. It was considered to be, from that hanging jury, the equivalent of acquittal. The fact that seaman Demara had defended himself and won such a verdict was considered, even more, to be the greatest thing done by an enlisted man since "Manila John" Bassiloni won the Medal of Honor.

He was, for perhaps the second time in his life, a hero— with mitigating circumstances, of course.

Fred Demara served his term (cut down on review to eighteen months because of good attitude and behavior) "standing on his head," as is said about an easy stretch. He was sent to Navy disciplinary barracks at San Pedro, California, where one of the first people he met was the editor of the camp newspaper who was about to be sprung. A few days later, when asked about his occupational background, he told them, naturally, that he was an ex-newspaperman. It came as no surprise to him when a few weeks later he was called in and asked to edit the camp newspaper, a little puff nicely called *Tars and Bars.*

Even in prison there was an innate, built-in American respect for freedom of the press.

"They let me go any place. That's where I learned about prison maintenance. When I left there I knew enough about it to run the place. Better than it was run, I mean."

His rehabilitation was considered to be so effective that the Army, when they finally caught up with Demara while at San Pedro, dropped charges. After a year and a half in jail Demara was given his discharge—dishonorable—and a one-way ticket to New York, which was where he had been enlisted.

Before going back home he decided to give life a try in Los Angeles. "Where else in America could a big fake hope to do better?" he asks. It didn't work out.

"I reeked and stank of con. I don't know how. Outside I looked like thousands of other guys. They must read it in the eyes and the way you react to a cop. Every time I leaned over to tie a shoelace, some cop was there saying, 'All right, Max, let's keep shoving that little ol' ass right along, Max, just keep moving till you're out of *this* town, Max. Now get.' "

He hadn't wanted to, but he wrote a letter home asking if they would have him, never sure that anyone was still alive there when he wrote. The letter from home was warm and reassuring.

What bothered him most was not being Dr. French.

"As Dr. French, those cops wouldn't have treated me that way. I really hated not being French. No. What I hated most was being Demara again. Who was Demara? Anyway you looked at it, French was somebody, good or bad. Good *or* bad, Demara—that guy was a bum."

He took a bus East, determined to quit the life he was living. The only long-range answer to his life was to make Demara amount to something. Somewhere outside of Cincinnati, the bus took on a young man who turned out to be a student at Asbury College, a small 1,000-student school near Lexington, Kentucky. The boy kept talking about his wonderful teacher, a professor named Dr. Cecil Boyce Hamann, a doctor in biology from Purdue.

In answer to why such a brilliant man was at Asbury, the boy said the doctor liked the quiet, small-town life. "He's very quiet and very shy. Never goes *any place* but he sure knows his stuff."

Against his better judgment and against his will, Fred Demara found himself filing this intriguing information away in some dark corner of his mind.

14

THE SHORT LIFE OF
CECIL BOYCE HAMANN

As prodigal sons go, he got as good a reception in Lawrence as he could have expected.

"I have only this to say. I have paid my debt and now I am clear. But some of the places I was in and some of the things I did would have made you proud of me."

Since he had gone away the family had moved to State Street into a smaller house, much smaller than the one on Andover Road and backing directly on the railroad tracks. It greatly depressed him.

Ever since he'd conducted his own defense he had become convinced that his great future lay in the law and he evolved a plan. He would go to Boston and study law by day and pay for it by working at night. His family were pleased. It did not occur to them that a person with a criminal record need not apply to the bar, but it did to Demara. He had a way around that one.

Before leaving for Boston he did a characteristic thing. In his backyard he painted a large sign and then had it carried out to the edge of town where he put it up at night.

WELCOME TO LAWRENCE
Our motto: See Dante's *Inferno*, Canto III, Line 9

"For all I know the sign's still there. You don't think anyone in Lawrence ever bothered to look up the line, do you? But I'll bet a lot of out-of-towners got a hell of a laugh later."

The line is: *All hope abandon, ye who enter here.*

He took a large, gloomy, cheap room under his real name, on Commonwealth Avenue, and then he found a nighttime job in the Massachusetts General Eye and Ear Infirmary. For at least one reason it was the ideal situation. At night he had access to various offices and to the mailroom. Using Mass. General stationery and the forged signatures of Mass. General doctors, Demara began piling up the credentials of the quiet professor he had heard about on the bus. It was simple to find out where to start looking for credentials. He wrote to Dr. Cecil Boyce Hamann and asked him. It was his easiest job of getting the right background. At night he wrote his letters to the various institutions and colleges and in the morning he plucked any answers out of the mailbox of the doctor's name he had used.

In September, now owning almost every document ever issued to Hamann, Demara presented himself as a candidate for first-year law courses at Northeastern Law School as C. B. Hamann.

"I still feel I was on the right track. Even if I didn't make a great lawyer, the way I was heading I figured any little knowledge of briefs and torts was going to come in very handy."

Outside of doing well at law school his aim was to get married that year and begin raising a family.

"I tried *very* hard. I learned to dance. I told charming stories. I spent every cent I had on women. I think they liked me. I liked them. But nothing—nothing happened at all. You know why?" he asks. "Love is something real and I was a fake, and all of us must have sensed that. It didn't work."

He did better at Northeastern. But although his grades were good, he was driven to despair by boredom,

"There were times there when I thought I was losing my mind. No wonder most lawyers are so boring. It's a plot. Only one of their own beastly boring breed can suffer through those schools."

And he was unhappy at Mass. General. It was the same old curse that had helped start him on the way. Because of his limited background, as Demara there were no openings in advanced work. He remained a lab clean-up man.

Although he hadn't planned anything he knew his subconscious was making plans for him when he found himself, as Dr. Hamann, becoming a convert once again so that Hamann's letter of testimony would come from Boston. The feeling was heightened when he found it irresistible to pass up a handful of bishop's stationery when he paid a call on Bishop Wright. This he felt to be poetic justice, however, since it was mainly Wright who had been responsible for exposing French's credentials when he was at Subiaco.

Such activity almost always meant that Demara's mind was turning back to thoughts of religion and the Church.

One day, at the end of the summer of 1950, Demara closed his room on Commonwealth and headed for Alfred, Maine, where he appeared unannounced at the Brothers of Christian Instruction.

Would they be interested in a convert who was a Ph. D. from Purdue and who was a zoölogist whose specialty was cancer research?

The brothers were overwhelmed. So overwhelmed, in fact, that Demara then announced that he would be delighted to join their humble order if they could meet certain stipulations, most of which concerned his academic freedom and right to function in his field in his own way. They had no objections.

"I had learned things from St. Martin's. I didn't want people looking over my shoulder any more. My kind of teaching needs privacy," he explains. "Lots of privacy."

The first thing to capture his attention was the Notre Dame Normal School, a small junior college run by the brothers to educate their own candidates before sending them out as teachers mainly to French-Canadian parochial schools.

"The basic structure was there. Why not make it a full-time, formal four-year college? We could make it the Notre Dame of the North. That was my plan. 'Expand into the vacuum,' you know."

He began an unsubtle campaign for this from his first week there. The elder provincial council thought Brother John Payne extraordinarily pushy, but they had to admit even that had its points. There was, for example, the famous highway case. One afternoon a truckload of construction engineers arrived at the institute's campus and began surveying the old asphalt road.

"Oh, dear, they're finally going to build the highway through instead of going around," the provincial sadly said.

"Not if I can help it," Demara said grandly. No one at the school knew exactly how he managed it, but it involved several telephone calls to powerful people in Portland (who, it later turned out, thought he was calling for the bishop) and, when he talked to the engineers, the snub end of his automatic was sticking out of a fold in his cassock.

"You get off this property by the time I get back here," Brother John said, "or I'll shoot you off. Whose word do you think they'll take in court—mine, or some sinning bastard like you?"

They left. After that, Brother John, the man of the world, became a kind of school trouble-shooter. When a young brother didn't feel he could go back to the University of Montreal and finish his graduate courses, Brother John handled that one. He picked up the brother and by brute force carried him out to the order's station wagon, in which he drove all night to Montreal. The reluctant brother was deposited in class the next morning. Unethical it was, and effective too.

He became known as a wit and raconteur and a teller of risqué stories. Many orders of nuns have such names as The Poor Sisters of St. Francis Seraph of the Perpetual Adoration or The School Sisters of the Third Order of St. Francis (Panhandle, Texas). Demara amused the congrega-

tion by making up off-color titles such as The Pregnant Sisters of the Quick Conception (Paris, France).

"I must have been quite the wit. My best joke, though, was
one that's now famous all over the Church. It will give you an
idea of high jinks in the religious orders. It goes this way:
'What are the three questions that even God in all *His* wis-
dom can't answer?' And the reply is:

" 'How many orders of nuns are there in the world? Who
are smarter—the Jesuits or the Dominicans? How much
money do the Franciscans have?' It *always* got a great big
laugh," Demara adds.

Demara's enthusiasm for founding the new college was
gaining adherents. The provincial and brothers began to be
persuaded that if they were ever going to carry out their
function in this world they had to THINK BIG. In the middle of all this he was informed that the time had come for
him to report to the novitiate. As if this alone weren't bad
enough, he learned that the novice house was situated in a
farm house somewhere between St. Leonard and Grand
Falls, New Brunswick, some three hundred frosty miles north
of Portland, Maine.

"Napoleon had his Elba, MacArthur his Bataan and
Hamann his Grand Falls. I shall return," he vowed.

He nearly didn't. "It was a fantastic place. They had me,
Dr. Hamann, out in the potato patches digging spuds at ten
below zero. They didn't seem to get the point that they were
risking the life of a great cancer researcher and future college president."

The boredom that might have crushed him was made
bearable by founder fever. He kept a steady stream of excited correspondence flowing between Grand Falls and
Alfred and, then, in mid-winter, he was called down to Augusta to appear before the state legislature's Committee on
Education to argue why the Institute Notre Dame should be
allowed a charter by the state to open a four-year university.
One other antidote to boredom was visiting the office of

young, Harvard-educated Dr. Joseph Cyr. Winter-locked in
the almost snow-bound village the two men became close
friends, and Demara mined the young doctor for medical
information. Near the end of his novitiate year, Brother John
was asked by Cyr if he could be of any help in getting him a
license to practice in the States.

"You give me your records and credentials, and I can,
Doctor," Demara said. "All of them. The more, the quicker."

Dr. Cyr went into the next room and began sorting
through piles of papers.

"Put in everything," Demara called in. "Baptism, confirmation, high school grades. Everything."

Cyr soon returned with a packet of papers that weighed
nearly a pound. "I did what you told me," he said.

"I don't think you'll have reason to regret it."

Demara swears he had no intention of ever using the—
to an impostor—almost priceless windfall that weighed
heavy in his hand.

When Demara returned to Alfred he was met with exhilarating news. The charter had been granted and the Brothers
of Christian Instruction were preparing to make Demara's
dream a quick reality. Demara could barely restrain himself.

"It was important to look cool and impartial. I didn't think
there was any doubt as to who would be the first rector. (I
personally preferred the title chancellor but that could be
changed later.) It was my enthusiasm and my idea and,
furthermore, I was the only one there with adequate degrees
to head a new college. (I preferred university.) But you
couldn't look greedy."

On a cheerless morning in spring Demara heard running
steps in the hall by his door. "They've posted the notice,
Brother John," a brother said, and set fly for the main house.

The notice was to be the listing of assignments for the
opening of the new school. Demara wanted desperately to
break into a run to the bulletin board but contented himself

with walking fast. It wouldn't do for the future chancellor to be seen running like a schoolboy.

He still finds it both hard and painful to believe what his eyes revealed to him.

His name was not at the top of the list, nor even near the top. Brother John Payne was listed as an instructor in biology.

"Not even head of the department," he cried out. "There must be a mistake."

The brothers around the bulletin board turned to eye him.

"What are you staring at?" he asked in a rage. "You know what the idiots have done." He pulled the list off the board over the protests of the others and shredded it.

"I swear to God that if I had had some dynamite and had known how to use it, I would have blown LaMennais College—that was the idiotic name they were planning for *my* school—off the face of the earth."

His rage was a combination of hot tears and cold, incensed anger. What bothered him most was the man who was chosen to head the school.

"Listen to me," he cried. "He's an idiot. A moron. He'll ruin you all," he screamed as he went to his room to pack. On his way back he passed the sacristy, where he stepped in for a bottle of sacristy wine.

"Brother, you can't do that. You . . ." a sexton said.

"Who's man enough around this dump to stop me?" He tilted the bottle to his lips and drained the quart in two swallows, which made him feel considerably better.

He came out and passed a station wagon in which a brother was sitting. He felt an impulse of quaint native cunning possess him.

"Did they fix it yet?" he asked the brother.

"Fix what?" the puzzled man asked.

"That whirring noise like the transmission is about to explode. Don't you hear it *inside?*" The brother shook his head that he didn't. "Then you'd better get out and listen. I'll race the motor for you."

When he was in the car, behind the wheel, he motioned the brother over.

"Now, pay attention," he said. "Tell them this. Say I hope their rotten college will prove such a failure that the crash will be heard all the way into the Vatican. Tell them someday they'll recognize the greatness of their error." He shifted the car into gear and began gliding away. "Now look out," he said kindly.

"That boy established the all-time doubletake. He just looked and looked and looked, his eyes growing wider and wider, as I went away. I believe I was halfway to New Hampshire before he cried 'Thief.' "

He wound his way eventually to Boston, where, on a whim, he parked the car in the exact parking lot and, he feels, spot that he parked his first stolen car.

"You always lose money on me," Demara told the parking man who just looked at him.

He went then as before to the Olde Union Oyster House and had a good meal. He thought about that time years before when he had last been there. He was older now. The glass of wine didn't go to his head and there wasn't the same thrill of being part of a conspiracy. There was the story of his escapade on page three, but it didn't move him too much. That sort of thing was getting old. Chiefly the thing that made him unhappy was the knowledge that after all these years he was exactly where the young boy had left off. He had no future.

Brazenly he registered for a room in the YMCA under his own name. He sat in the bleak light on the edge of his bed, depressed and regretful, when his hand felt the tight wad of papers he had been carrying around for weeks—the life and history of one Dr. Cyr.

He slipped off the rubber bands and let the papers drop one by one onto the drab white bedspread, and to him they looked like gold certificates. Birth certificate, transcript of grades from Laval Medical School in Quebec, medical license to practice in Canada and many more.

"I picked them up and let them flutter down on the bed. They were like miraculous little doves sent down from heaven to help me."

He swept the papers together and checked out of the hotel. He went across town to the venerable Parker House where he registered with a flourish. The clerk handed his key to the bellhop.

"Take Dr. Cyr to seven eighteen, please. Doctor, have a pleasant stay with us, sir."

"I'm certain I shall," he said, in the grand manner.

"Right this way, Doctor," the bellhop said, and it was good to be servilely spoken to again.

The room was excellent and his window looked out over that Boston Common. Now, this is more like it, he thought.

Although the Common lay buried in snow, devoid of people, strangely unmoving and dead beneath the sterility of the lights that wind their way through that park, he felt he could feel the greenness and life of the grass that lay just beneath the crust of snow.

Life was just as hopeful, just as stirring, just as full of promise as it ever had been. He picked up the house phone.

"This is Dr. Cyr's room. Will you send me up a bottle of soda and a fifth of Scotch? I think I'm going to have a little party."

He sat by the window, sipping his drinks, until he felt mellowly drunk. "But who was it that said there wasn't any future? Someone called Demara," he said aloud to himself and went peacefully to bed.

15

In the second week of March, in 1951, Demara boarded a
bus in Boston and headed north to St. John, New Brunswick.
He had never felt quite as unsure about anything in his life
before. His aim was to present himself for a commission as a
doctor in the Royal Canadian Navy. He had no idea what
the procedures were or what he might expect. He had nothing, in fact, except Dr. Cyr's documents. He chose St. John
because it was in Cyr's home province and so wouldn't excite
curiosity and yet was far enough away from Grand Falls so
that the chances of anyone knowing Cyr were not too great.

On March 13, tired, hungry and nearly penniless, he appeared in the doorway of a Royal Canadian Navy recruiting
office.

"I am Dr. Joseph Cyr of this province and I feel it is my
duty, now that we are again in war, to volunteer my services
where they can be of most help."

The Korean war was then underway in some of its blood-
ier phases. The rating in the recruiting office was duly impressed. He was something more than that, he was flabbergasted. At that time Navy system of recruiting qualified doctors for service was getting perilously close to a policy of
shanghaiing doctors off the street at night. The recruiting
petty officer was not even sure how exactly to go about it.

"Now wait there, sir. *Please*. Sit right down. Get nice
and warm there. Don't make a move," he said, while he
scurried out to make a hasty phone call to a superior officer.

The officer who came back with the enlisted man was equally impressed and eager to please.

"You're going to love it in the RCN, Dr. Cyr. Fine organization and a fine body of men, sir."

That evening Demara was placed aboard a special Navy plane and flown to Ottawa, and on the very next afternoon he was presented before the medical officer selection board. The Royal Canadian Navy denies that Demara was given any extra red-carpet treatment and that might well be, but it would seem apparent that he at least was given some very extra-special red-tape cutting. There was a cursory check made of Cyr's documents and those were assuredly in complete and grand order. Demara feels that the chief thing decided was that he would make an acceptable officer, gentleman and especially messmate, despite his being a French-Canadian. Dr. Cyr, big, friendly, red of face and strong of hand, was obviously made in the mold of the British bulldogs and was officer's mess material. He was asked a series of rather general questions which, far from having anything to do with medicine, were directed toward finding out if he was a radical practitioner who might just be thinking of using the RCN boys as practice patients to perfect his surgery or as potential proof of any theories. They found that Dr. Cyr had no strong or advanced theories about anything in medicine. They also wanted to find his feelings about socialized medicine, and when he launched into a ringing defense of free enterprise the interview was over.

"I wasn't afraid *then*," Demara says. "It was clear that they didn't call people to Ottawa for a medical quiz. That would be aimless. They mainly wanted to see where you would fit into the service.

He was returned to St. John, where he was entered into the Royal Canadian Navy and commissioned a surgeon lieutenant. The next few days he spent in extended meetings with the best Navy tailor on St. John getting himself perfectly fitted into several sets of dark-blues for winter and several pairs of dashing summer whites. On March 19, only nine days after he had driven out of Alfred in a stolen car, Demara was formally assigned to duty in the RCN hospital in the big east coast navy port of Halifax.

At his arrival in Halifax he was greeted coolly by a senior medical officer and eyed suspiciously by the doctors who would be working with him. He had his first moment of terror. They had to have some piece of advance information, he felt, that made them act so coolly toward him. He didn't know then that the officers in his section were annoyed at being sent a Frenchie. At noon, as some of the doctors gathered for lunch, Demara felt the chill of the room as people eyed him silently.

"I don't suppose *you'd* care for a little drink before lunch," an officer finally said. "You'd prefer wine, I suppose."

"I wouldn't care for a little drink, no. But I would care for a big one."

It wasn't very much of a joke but it broke the tension. He didn't talk with an accent, at least. After several good, stiff drinks, during which it was established that Cyr was half-Irish and all man and a regular guy for the mess, Lieutenant Cyr was accepted.

Demara's first duty was to take sick call each morning at the base. This can, of course, if a patient reports in with something like spinal meningitis, be a terribly important responsibility. Demara did a smart thing. He went to his superior, as an enlightened, intellectually curious, eager man with a problem.

"I've been asked by some people to work up a rule of thumb guide for the people in lumber camps. Most of them don't have doctors handy and they're pretty isolated. Could we get together a little guide that would pretty well cover most serious situations?"

To the lieutenant's superior, as Demara had hoped, this was a challenge and a pleasure. For two days he went through his books, culling and refining a basic code for the amateur diagnostician, and finally gave it to Demara.

"How does *that* look?" he asked proudly.

"Gosh, doctor, I think it's great. You really know your medicine and how to get it across to the layman. This is great."

And so it was. Demara made a copy of the code and followed it faithfully. This, as far as he knows, guided him correctly through most of his Navy career. And then, he was sold on antibiotics. Whenever he saw a sore throat, heard a serious-sounding cough or saw someone who looked very bad, he rammed them full of penicillin and, after that, with whatever miracle drugs happened to be current and choice. If the patient persisted in staying sick, Fred would manage to maneuver him to any one of six or seven other doctors, using each one as sparingly as possible.

"What do you think of this one, Bill?" he would ask, and the doctor, after his own examination, would give his opinion. Demara always took it.

He had a fond and complete hope that before the year was over he would have absorbed enough medical knowledge to put him on par with all but the great doctors.

In May, however, Demara was shifted to duty on HMCS *Magnificent*, the great aircraft carrier, which was anchored out in Halifax Bay. The procedure here was different. There was no other doctor to question. There was only a rather stiff, stern Command Medical Officer who would come around each evening, quickly examine some of the more serious patients, and then examine Surgeon Lieutenant Cyr's suggested and carried out treatments. There was not much way to fake that. The CMO was not impressed with his new junior officer.

Lieutenant Cyr, he wrote in a report, "lacked training in medicine and surgery, especially in diagnosis."

Through the service grapevine Demara eventually heard of the CMO's uncomplimentary report and he resolved to do something about it. He devised a marvelous system.

Any patient about whom he wasn't certain or who seemed to offer complications, he hid.

Without bothering to tell anyone higher than a responsible bosun's mate, he commandeered several seamen's rooms down in the bowels of the ship. On these he tacked up quarantine signs and into them he put his questionable patients. He operated on the theory that God was on the side of the big battalions and doctors who used quarts of penicillin.

"Swamp the enemy, was my motto," he says.

If any of them had happened to die down there, it could have been immensely embarrassing.

"I had thought about that, believe me. I wasn't going to let that happen but it did worry me."

"Before I took the job I had done my research and one thing made me feel better. With or without medical care, outside of war and accidents and such things as lung cancer, no one—no strong man actually dies any more."

Under this new system Cyr's accomplishment record improved so rapidly and considerably that other doctors once more took him seriously. It was assumed that, unused to being checked on, he had suffered a spate of "buck fever."

On a warm, surprising day in June something happened to Demara that he had been dreading would happen at the wrong time and place. It was late in the month and the first day that officers wore whites. As he meticulously dressed in his fresh, new whites he was aware that he had never looked better in his life. He had lost some weight and compulsory exercise sessions had kept him in good shape. In the early afternoon, since he was off-duty, he decided to take the *Magnificent* launch into Halifax harbor.

The wind was from the south and the day was warm, which in Canada has a special rich feeling. The sea was soft, and ashore, where clumps of dirty snow had lurked only days before, the grass was green. He stood near the bow and had that especially wonderful feeling of being all put together properly.

Here he was in truth an officer and gentleman in the Royal Canadian Navy going about on the business of His Royal Highness, the King. He was of a breed—the junior officers who had made England what it was, going about the world subduing savages, making the world safe for investors and spreading the empire in such a way that the sun could no longer find a way to set on it.

As he went through the drab streets of Halifax he felt he glittered as he walked.

Sunshine, surprising and rich with the texture of liquid, washed the bricks of the harbor houses, and the park, when he passed, was bathed in the goldness of it. The green of the grass, greening against the lemon drops of dandelions and banks of unfulfilled daffodils, was the insideness of green, and on it, composed and quiet, a Navy nurse sat.

She was serene and calm and beautiful and he fell in love with her at once.

He climbed over the low iron fence and began trotting toward her as if they had had a date of long standing, and only when he stood in front of her did he realize that she wasn't looking back at him and that he had nothing to say. He finally knelt down beside her and picked a dandelion.

"The most underrated flower in the world," he said, and he was delighted and thrilled when she smiled that she might agree.

"Most flowers taper to the top. Very common. Dandelion leaves spread out as they climb. Very unusual."

She didn't answer but it didn't frighten him. There was no need to talk or answer and that was the way she handled it. Finally she said, "Do you know what the word means?"

He thought for a moment and said, "It's from the French. *Dande de lion,* mane of the lion, because the flower looks like the mane of the lion."

She laughed sweetly and the sound of it reminded him

of the movie *Heidi* and little bells that had tinkled in the snow when it was clear and frosty.

"That's really very imaginative of you," she said. "It's *dent de lion*, tooth of the lion, because of the jagged leaves. But yours is much better."

It was and he said so and she was pleased that he wasn't falsely modest.

"I like them because they're so sturdy," the nurse said. "And reliable. I'm from northern Alberta and we never could count on anything. A sudden snow would come or a freeze and all the flowers would die but when the snow melted, there they were, the dandelions."

"I want to be reliable," he said. It sounded strange. "I want to be reliable. I want someone to rely on me."

"Yes, that is nice, to have someone rely on you," she said. Her voice was as soft and calm as the light of the sun coming through the thin green of the lilac leaves.

"We used to play that if you could blow all the fluff off a dandelion you got your wish," Demara said.

"We used to say it meant you were in love," she said.

"No, no. You've got that wrong. You hold the dandelion under someone's chin and if it makes the chin all yellow, he's in love."

He watched her pick another flower and he was impressed by the long, strong gentleness of her hands. She held the flower under his chin.

"Did you know you were in love?"

"Oh, yes," he said fervently. "I've been deeply in love for minutes. Wait," he said. He seized her wrist as she was getting up.

It was silly, he knew, but he felt it was terribly important that the dandelion shine yellow on her chin. He turned her face directly into the sun and held the flower beneath her chin. His hands were trembling, but there was the shimmering of faint pale gold reflected against the soft whiteness of her throat. He pulled her to her feet.

"Well? What did it show?" she asked.

They waded through the softness of the grass and he enjoyed the moment of waiting.

"Oh, you're in love. It was very yellow. You are very much in love."

"Isn't that nice." She took his hand and he wasn't surprised.

"Now, let's have lunch. A small place. A French place. We'll have a bottle of wine and a . . . Oh, it's Friday, isn't it? Are you Catholic?"

She nodded that she was.

"And isn't *that* nice. So am I. A bottle of wine, then, and a fish."

As they walked he made a most determined vow that this woman was a person he was never going to lie to. And he made a vow to return to the Church.

"I think you should know one thing before we go any farther. My real name is Fred W. Demara, and I'm an American but in the Navy they call me . . ."

"No, no, please don't," she was saying. "I want to save that. I want to fall in love and not even know my lover's name."

"It is fun. I wish you'd listen, though."

"Do you know what I'd like?" she said. She leaped over the rail fence in one swift, incredibly graceful movement. "I'd like to run into someone I know, my superior, and say, 'I'd like you to meet the man that I love. Lieutenant . . . ah, lieutenant. *What* is your name, Lieutenant?'"

That afternoon the citizens of Halifax were treated to the unusual sight of two Royal Navy officers dancing down the streets of town, hand in hand, singing at the top of their voices something about falling in love being wonderful. And it was.

16

For the first time that he could remember, outside of the rather vague hopes of becoming a bishop, he had a definite plan and goal. His aim was to last out his time of service in the Navy and when he got his discharge to settle down in some out-of-the-way Canadian town—perhaps in northern Alberta, where Catherine came from (that was, he found, the name of his love), and become a general practitioner. The chances of ever meeting anyone out of the past there, except out of the Canadian Navy, were remote. His own past would also be legitimate—it would be the Navy.

His interest in medicine also became a compulsion. In Demara's favor was the fact that when he wasn't courting Catherine he was studying medical books, trying in a few months' time to make up for the four years of medical school he never attended. He was known as a kind of good-natured bookworm.

The thing that most troubled him was that he was continually amazed that this girl could like him, much less love him. The old line would not let him alone; love is something real and genuine and he was neither. He began to doubt the genuineness of his love and to challenge it. It made him unhappy and Catherine unhappy.

He also respected her as he had never before respected anyone. He was eager to reveal to her the truth of his life and then if she would or could still have him, he would be freed to begin a new life with her. As it was now, she was in love with Joe Cyr, not with Fred Demara.

He had to tell her and he didn't know how.

And there was a final complication. Catherine was due to be discharged from the service and, as women in love are wont to feel, she wanted to be married—soon.

This he couldn't do. He refused to marry her as Cyr. He had a morbid fear of being sent to Korea and being killed in action and then being uncovered as an impostor when he couldn't defend himself. And last was the not inconsiderable dread that the local newspaper publicity would not only expose him but land him in jail.

Who was in love with Catherine, anyway? Was it the Navy officer handsome and clean in his whites or was it really the dismal failure from the dismal Massachusetts mill town? When he went up the aisle of a church with his bride-to-be on his arm, would he really be getting married or would this just be another mockery by the Catholic who had been excommunicated so many times that it was a miracle that Satan hadn't yet made a personal trip out of the sulphur pits to collect his choice new trophy?

He began to dread dying or being alone with Catherine or talking to her. Morbidly he began to drink heavily, not getting drunk but becoming swathed in its protective vapors as if he were wrapping himself in a cocoon. Catherine didn't seem to notice. She was so caught up in the world that lay ahead of them, she glowed with exuberance, and she radiated such simple faith and charm when she talked that his tongue simply wouldn't move.

"Now, what was it you were so eager to talk about, darling?" she would ask and it took all of his will power to thickly mumble, "Nothing, nothing at all," and excuse himself to pour another drink so that he wouldn't feel the sharpness of the turmoil moiling around inside his mind and heart.

For Demara there was, as much as he regretted it, only one solution, one he had used so often before that he turned to it instinctively without planning it. Escape.

Feeling like an evil reprobate but operating automatically he went down to Naval headquarters and there he begged to be sent into action in Korea at once. Maybe there the solution would come. Perhaps he could write Catherine the truth and let the hurt come at a distance. Perhaps he might even get himself killed.

One unfortunate incident marred things. When he had requested absolute secrecy about his volunteering for overseas action the Navy had felt that the doctor was simply being modest. His voluntary-exile notice was posted in several of the medical officer's messes around Halifax as an example to prod the rest of the desk-bound slackers.

When, the next time he saw Catherine, he looked into her eyes he knew that she knew.

"How could you have done it? How could you without telling me?"

He put his arms around her and let her cry until he felt her finally stopping.

"It's something only a man can explain," he began softly. "I enlisted in the service to help some cause. I can't even name it. But I know this. I could never be to you but half a man until I had faced up to my duty and done it."

She refused to understand.

"Then let me try it this way. I've never talked much about my past, have I?"

He had put his first foot in and wondered if perhaps this wasn't the drastic time to go all the way, but when she pulled away from him and studied his face with her tear-filled eyes, a resolution he had felt was cast of iron was found to be made of tinsel.

"Someone in my family, someone very close to myself was a deserter from both the Army and the Navy. For years now I have felt it was my duty—you might even say my destiny, to avenge that shame and guilt."

Catherine wavered.

"Until I can say I've seen my duty and I've done it, I'm no

real good to myself and no good to you. No one can say what a man's limits are when a matter of honor is involved."

She capitulated. "I think I understand, dear," she said and then he heard himself talking again.

"One more thing. I have this premonition that I'm going to be killed. Saints come to me in visions at night and beg me not to include you in the tragedy of my life."

She was staring at him with fear and anger.

"Then that's all the more reason why I have to marry you. I must marry you, Joe, please. I must."

He had committed an awful blunder. Having victory in his grasp and the ground controlled, he made one last foray and found himself cut off with no method of retreat. And for once he couldn't attack. She attacked him.

In the days that followed that scene, she either begged him for marriage or threatened to leave him, neither of which he could face or bear.

"If you can't find it in the bigness of your heart to love both me and your country then I want you to know that, even though I love you, I will try my best to find a man who can."

"Now, Catherine," he would say in a terrified way, "you can't mean that and you don't mean it."

"But I do," she would say calmly, and the worst was he knew she meant it.

He could hardly wait for his orders to come down. He began to haunt Halifax headquarters. "Please, please," he would beg, "will you get me out of this hellhole and out to Korea where I belong?"

It was a glorious day in August when Surgeon Lieutenant Joseph Cyr received his orders to report to CANAVHED (Naval Headquarters at Esquimalt, British Columbia) for assignment in Korean waters.

On the eve of his departure his messmates held a riotous party for him. There was, in its desperation to avoid a tragic scene, a sense of tense hilarity about the party. Everyone drank too much too fast and got too drunk except Catherine. It was still early in the evening when Demara discovered that the wardroom was empty of everyone but himself and Catherine. He was by now maudlin, teary-eyed and his resistance was decidedly low.

"Say you'll marry me," she whispered in his ear. "Make a promise now, Joe, darling. It's so easy." And her voice murmured in his ear with the gentle, comforting hum of richly laden honey bees.

"Now, say it after me. 'I love you, Catherine, and I will marry you,'" she rippled and babbled in his ear and he did. It was easy, really. He said it again and felt a sincere pleasure saying it, and before he really realized it—that only came to him in the morning when he woke—he knew he was saying "this morning."

Someone was shaking him. The messboy. "All right, Doc. Train's leaving in fifteen minutes."

Someone had taken his equipment down to the station, but all that he could remember was that he had to get married today, he had promised. At the station Catherine was already there waiting for him, crisp and fresh in her white uniform. He appeared to have served as an ash tray for the party.

"You haven't forgotten?" she asked.

"No, I haven't forgotten." It was strange, he felt, that she didn't cry when he finally boarded the train and he felt more than just a little hurt at her last words to him.

"Change into a fresh uniform and look pretty, dear," she said.

Strange words to leave with a man who was sailing away to war. He was relieved that she hadn't made a scene but then he did hope for something more than that. He was equally ashamed of the feeling of freedom and relief he experienced when the train was finally safely out of Halifax.

He had a good sleep and changed his rumpled uniform and he felt like a completely new man when the train slowed

down to begin edging into Montreal. He was eyeing the promising town with a growing sense of adventure when he
jumped halfway back across the aisle. There up ahead of
him, waiting at the tip of the landing platform, was Catherine.

With her were a group of people who had that homogene-
ous look that a solid family offers. Worst of all, with them was
a priest who had all the earmarks of being there on business.

He acted without thinking. While the train was still moving, he went to the opposite side of the train, and managed
to get one of the doors open and jump.

For an hour and a half he saw his lovely Catherine, trying
hard not to cry in front of her family, combing the station
and the platform eagerly and hopefully for him while he hid
in a grimy, cold part of a baggage loading shed. He cried.

What he had not counted on was her stubbornness. When
he clambered back on board the train, she was there, in
his seat, waiting for him.

"You were right, darling," she said. All of her tearfulness
was gone.

"It was a dirty trick, wasn't it?"

"It was a silly one but one that I love you for," he
answered.

Somewhere, somehow he had to tell the truth to this girl
and then he had to marry her and live happily ever afterward with her. She rode all the way to Winnipeg with him
before she had to leave and take a plane back to Halifax,
and they never were closer, or happier with each other.

"I know what you have to do," she said, "and I'm not going
to be looking for that man who can love both his country
and me at the same time. That was selfish, I see. I just love
you and want you to come back safely to me when you've
done your duty."

The pain and sorrow of that parting were so deep and ex-
quisite that he managed to get all the rest of the way across
Canada without seeing any part of it or without being able

to recall the trip. At Vancouver he took the ferry across the Strait of Georgia to Esquimalt.

"After you've done your duty." To do his duty—that was the thing now. He wanted desperately to do good and ye he was terrified of what he was stepping into.

At Esquimalt he got his duty. He was to report at onc to join His Majesty's Canadian Ship *Cayuga*—a destroyer —as medical officer. The lives of two hundred and eleven seamen and eight officers were in his hands.

"May God help us all now," he whispered when the order was put in his hand.

17

SURGEON CYR

TO THE COMBAT ZONE

On board the *Cayuga* they were equally worried. On a smal
ship, especially one going into combat waters, next in line
to the captain and the executive officer, the medical officer is
the most speculated-about officer on board. On any of these
three at any time a man's life may depend. It is the men's un-
spoken hope that they will get a feeling of authority and confidence from all three.

Also, on a small ship the officers' mess becomes a very
close and private thing. One misfit can spoil an entire voyage
or tour of duty. The officers were as worried about the newcomer as the men were.

Although the Canadian Navy is representative of all of
Canada it still is very heavy with the British tradition. There
remains much of the "jolly good show" attitude, and the British bulldog breed of gentleman, the rugger playing regular
officer, is still a type much in demand in the mess. More than
was the ordinary case this was true on the *Cayuga*. The news
that one Joe Cyr, Frenchman, was coming on board was
greeted with gloom.

When Surgeon Lieutenant Cyr was piped on board almost
all of the ship's complement was massed on board, straining
for a first look.

"For a frog he's a big enough bastard, isn't he?" Demara
heard one seaman say. They weren't given much of a chance
to study him. Someone, who later turned out to be the executive officer, took him by the arm.

"Excuse me, Doctor, but will you come with me to the captain's cabin at once? The old man's in real pain."

Demara noted a sudden sinking sensation in the region around his heart, a sensation that was becoming endemic with him. The captain was sick. They wound along the passageway and up a companionway oblivious to the stares of the seamen. Outside the captain's door he took a deep swallow of air and went in.

"Lieutenant Cyr," the exec said, "this is your new captain, Commander Plomer."

Demara started to smile. The sight of the captain made him want to go into a dance. The commander's jaw was swollen the size of a small melon. He obviously was the victim of several infected teeth.

"Glad haff you board," the commander managed to mumble. "Now pull these damn things. Thass order."

"Now, now," Demara said in what he hoped was his best bedside manner. He peered into the officer's mouth. "I'll just zip down to my quarters and arrange my gear, sir. Have them out in a jiffy."

Once in the passageway he *did* do a jig. A few older people in New England still refer to such liveliness as a tittup, and that is what Demara was doing. He pranced and capered down the companionway.

"The bloody bastard's not only big, he's loony," he heard the same seaman say. He made a note to get him at some future date, such as at inoculation time. He also ceased tittuping.

Once in his cabin he began arranging his gear, whistling casually as he did so, when it occurred to him that he didn't have the very least idea of how to properly pull a tooth. With an enlisted man, he hated to admit to himself, he might have risked experimenting. With Commander Plomer it behooved him to do it right—the first time.

The more he thought about it, the more concerned he got. He wasn't even certain that he could spot an infected tooth.

He wasn't sure which instrument to use. He didn't know if he had any novocaine in his emergency kit and he had no idea how to use it if he did.

"Can I be of any help?" the exec asked.

"Thank you, no," Demara said. "I prefer to work alone. Reduces the chances of infection." He pointed abruptly toward the door. He hated to be abrupt, but it wasn't going to do to have the second in command see him reading medical books to find how to pull a tooth. The moment the door clicked shut, he made a leap for his books.

There was, amazingly enough to him, not a single word about teeth. In growing desperation he scanned the indexes and when he found no reference to teeth and pulling of same, he turned to face, head, jaw in hopes of finding the light.

He turned suddenly, feeling he was being watched, to see a group of seamen curiously watching him through his porthole.

"Get away from there," he shouted. He pulled the blind. God knows what *they* were thinking, he thought.

There was a pounding at the door. "The Commander says to *please* hurry," a voice came through it. "What is the trouble, he says?"

"No trouble, no trouble. My medical gear is disorganized. Tell him to hold on for another minute or two."

The minute stretched out into an interminable quarter of an hour. Still Demara leafed through pages, by now not really looking but merely doing something to stop from thinking.

"Are you all right in there?" the exec roared. "The captain *orders* you to come."

"I'll be right out. Please respect my position," he scolded. "I am doing the best I can."

He stared at the door wondering when they would come in and take him to the skipper. There was no longer any avoiding the dilemma. He got out a syringe and, luckily, found novocaine. The directions were almost impossible for him to understand.

He could hear people milling out in the passageway, grumbling and impatient, and he had to experiment and practice squirting novocaine while his hands trembled. He loaded the hypodermic to the top, seized the largest pair of forceps he could find, and started for the door.

"Oh Captain! My Captain! our fearful trip is done"—before it ever began, he recalls thinking.

"Open up the door," someone called, and pounded on the door. As they did, he opened it, coming perilously close to being hit in the face by a fist. "I come," he said.

Few men have ever trod a path even to Tyburn tree with more tarrying tred.

"What in the bloody hell's the matter, anyway?" the exec demanded. "It's only a tooth, isn't it, Doc?"

"It's a lot more than that, I fear," Demara said sadly.

In Plomer's office he went directly to the captain, forced open his jaws and began to operate. *"Whush that?"* Plomer managed to gasp when his eye caught the syringe.

"Look, Commander. You run your ship, I'll run my sick bay. Right?"

"Right," he said.

He let loose the contents of the syringe and waited. The commander's face showed no reaction at all, but then, Demara figured, it was hard to tell with those professional salts. He might even then be passing on to another world but still be smiling all the way—a tight, little grim smile to be sure.

"Feel anything?" he asked. He tapped around the swollen area and then he tapped all around the officer's head. There was apparently no feeling anywhere. The time was ripe.

He took the forceps, found the obviously bad tooth and, wincing as he went, he pulled. It came so easily that he nearly went backward into the cabin's wall. The second came as easily. He went back to his room and waited but he heard nothing. Late the next morning he finally ventured out and his eye caught sight of the commander on the bridge.

"Good morning," Plomer boomed down. "I've been wanting to see you, Doctor."

Demara once again felt his heart plummet downward.

"Nicest job of tooth pulling I've ever had," Plomer cried. "Glad to have you aboard, Cyr."

"Prouder than ever to be aboard, sir," Fred said.

Demara was so relieved that that afternoon, he pulled what he feels is his very best joke of all time. He waited until the executive officer, who by now knew him, was on duty before appearing in the officers' mess. As he entered he greeted the assembled officers in French.

"Bonjour, mes officiers," he said. "Eet ees plaisaire meet you."

A few officers managed to mumble a subdued hello.

"Theese food," he said with disgust. "Eeet is no cook in wine, eh? Bah." At which point he began to slurp the food with a Gallic exaggeration that even Fernandel, the French movie clown, would not try to get away with.

"How many you people here French, eh? A bas with the pope haters, eh?"

There was a numbed silence in the room.

"Last place I make a lot of money chaging sailor money for medical treatment. How you guys make money?"

"Lieutenant, . . ." someone began, but Demara headed him off.

"I hope we no go to Korea, eh? Might get hurt. I scared. You plenty scared, too?"

They looked at him as if he were some pagan who had stumbled into the last Supper. Here was a frog to end all frogs. And then he began laughing. It started as a small chuckle but soon spread out into something gigantic and bellowing. In spite of themselves the other officers soon began to join in, infected by the laugh, unable to resist it. As they did so, they began to see the joke.

"Oh, my good God, the *looks* on your faces," he shouted. Tears were streaming down his face, and theirs by then.

From that moment on the *bon docteur* was accepted. He was in. His popularity as a messmate was instant and immense.

The same was true with the ratings. In the RCN there is an old tradition for handling troubles not quite severe enough to warrant court-martial called Captain's Mast. If they choose, the enlisted men can be represented at this kangaroo court by an officer who is then known as The Prisoner's Friend. It is either to his credit or discredit that Demara became almost exclusively among the officers The Prisoner's Friend.

"The reason for it was simple," he explains. "I wasn't afraid to lie like hell for the men. They appreciated that no end. I am a superior sort of liar. I don't tell any truth at all, so then my story has a unity of parts, a structural integrity and this way sounds more like the truth than truth itself."

He also was appointed officer in charge of the daily rum ration, a great honor for a newcomer since the handling of the daily grog ration is one of the most sacred rituals in the entire Navy experience.

The small ship sailed westward into the Pacific. The voyage out was easy and pleasant and remains to Demara one of the most pleasant things which ever happened to him. He studied constantly and he had the feeling that he was actually acquiring a solid body of medical knowledge. It was all beginning to take shape, and every piece seemed to suddenly find a niche.

He wrote exuberant, charming and delighted letters to Catherine, sorry now that they hadn't gotten married and planning their future ahead. He received equally exuberant answers to them.

In September the *Cayuga* reached Japan and stopped for refitting before going south and into Korean waters.

"You're hiding something, Doc," a rough chief petty officer said one day as they both leaned over the railing looking down into the dirty, cluttered waters of Kobe harbor. He came close to revealing that he was.

"You been in the American Navy, don't kid me. Every hunk of gear you name on this ship, you give a Yank name to. One, you wouldn't even know the name if you hadn't been in the Yank Navy. Two, you just wouldn't happen to give it that name. You know too much. Right, Doc?"

He was startled. How much had the men in the mess noticed? he wondered. Probably nothing. The thing to do with a man like this was to trust him.

"That's right, mate," he said. "But I don't like to talk about it. Understand." He gave him a manly wink.

"Got you," the mate said pleasantly, and Demara knew that man would never mention a word. "But that was a god damn choco-bar Navy, wasn't it? They really spoiled those boys. I was in it, too."

Those were the pleasant days, all right. Indian summer days in the warm, clear waters north of the 78th parallel.

A few days before the ship was to move down, another Canadian destroyer came into Kobe for repairs. It had taken a series of heavy artillery shells on its superstructure.

"How is it down there? For the Navy, I mean?" Demara asked.

"Oh, it's easy down there," an officer said. "But it can be rough. We're making these commando raids on shore installations. It isn't bad now but the gooks are going to get the hang of it. One of these days they're going to blow the whole flotilla into the East China Sea."

If his luck held true the *Cayuga* would be a part of it. He could see them taking forty or fifty seriously wounded casualties. Once again he experienced a sensation of having water in place of blood in his veins, and his heart was alternately beating in his throat and hiding in his shoes.

"God, do you know? I'm scared," he said.

"You ought to be," the officer assured him.

18

They drifted down along the east coast of Korea, north of the 38th parallel, keeping a check on North Korean shore operations. There was little to indicate at sea that somewhere among the stubby green pines that littered the hills, alone and in clumps, men of a great number of nations and rates were dying. Every so often the *Cayuga*, however, would turn broadside to the shoreline and for several hours blast away at fortified areas that concealed guns and men of the North Korean Army. After several weeks of this Dr. Cyr's apprehensions lessened. It was a quiet, almost lazy war in which the worst casualty he had been asked to treat was the burned hand of some seaman who forgot and picked up a red-hot shell casing.

With the *Cayuga*, which was guarding them, were several old Republic of Korea minesweepers and on them were parties of ROK commandos who were primed to make sudden landings and cause a good deal of devastation among shore installations. The *Cayuga* provided close-in artillery support. The landing barges were small, powered Korean junks. The attacks were usually made against unfortified places but sometimes against fortified ones; so sudden were they and so effective was the Canadian covering fire, that casualties were rare.

But every time he heard a weapon fired or heard the distant drumming of artillery from Korea, and any time he saw the flash of tracers light the sky he knew that the time of reckoning would come.

Late one afternoon in September, on a rough and choppy day, with the sea still running high following a two-day autumn blow and the *Cayuga*, a tiger of a ship, taking the heavy swells as well as any destroyer can take high seas— which is not very well—the *Cayuga's* lookout notified the bridge that something strange was taking place off the starboard side of the ship.

The bridge was able to pick up a small Korean junk which was frantically trying to establish some sort of contact with the *Cayuga*. Their fear was that it might be a trap, and with the help of a Korean liaison officer on board they blinked out a message telling the junk to stop her motors and then throw down her anchors. If it was a trap she at least was assured of dying in it.

As the ship pulled up close alongside the junk the men looked down at a pitiable sight. On the wet, matted floor of the junk, sprawled in filth and blood, lay a cargo of human bodies, every one of them to some degree mutilated. The men stared down for as long as most of them could take it and then turned away. In the junk they lay quiet.

"Jesus Christ," one sailor said. "Someone help them. Quick. Get Dr. Cyr."

"Get Dr. Cyr. Get Dr. Cyr," the men said.

"They were caught in ambush," the Korean explained. "Is there someone here who will help them, they want to know?"

"Is there?" he asked.

Commander Plomer had witnessed the grisly sight and was on his way to the sick bay where he had last seen the doctor. "I'll ask Joe and see if he wants to take them on."

What none of them knew was that Demara had already seen the cargo of dead and wounded and was on his way back down into the bowels of the ship. He wasn't running, he assured himself, but he was merely giving himself a chance to straighten himself out. Out of sight, out of mind, he hoped. Perhaps they'd go away. Perhaps Plomer would decide that it was illegal for him to operate on Koreans or decide that the *Cayuga* had better be moving and save the men by towing them to some more permanent installation. Whatever might happen, he wanted, if at all possible, to give it a chance to develop.

They found him down near the engine room.

"Good God, Joe," Gunnery Officer Little said. "Where in hell have you been? We've searched this ship high and low for you."

"Why, down here seeing the engine idle. I haven't had a chance before."

Strangely enough it sounded reasonable. And in that time he had decided what he would do.

Probably most of the men were not as badly wounded as they appeared to be. The ones who were mortally wounded would die with or without his manipulations. The others might die, but even crude minor surgery, backed by antibiotics, might keep them alive. No matter how many he might see die on the operating table and no matter how many he might kill, he still would be doing better than leaving them on the floor of the junk to die for sure.

"There's a bunch of ROK gooks in this junk, Doc. Man, it's a pitiful sight. I never saw worse and I seen plenty."

"Let's go," Dr. Cyr said dramatically. He rushed along the passageway, conscious of the men clearing way for him with that respect people always reserve for doctors in an emergency, and conscious of the whispers—"The doc's here. The doc's here. It's going to be all right. The doc's here."

"You willing, Joe?" Plomer asked. "It is not required."

He looked down at the men in the junk. Some of them must have been in great agony but none of them showed a trace of it. Most of them, he noted, were extremely young. Many of them were boys.

"Tell them," he heard Plomer say to the Korean liaison officer, "that the doctor's here. Tell them that they're going to be all right now, the doctor's here. You willing, Joe?" he asked Demara and even at that time he had to laugh.

"I don't think a doomed man has ever had less option. I'd better go down there now."

As he climbed over the side and looked down again, the men in the junk were smiling up at him. Their patience and courage in the face of pain and hopelessness still today remain his strongest memory of Korea.

"Let's get a litter brigade going here," he called up, feeling confident of himself for the first time. A little Korean in the boat began, in a harsh, guttural voice, to shout out orders and Demara was horrified to see the men in the junk begin to stagger to their feet and start stumbling and clawing their way up a rope ladder to the deck of the destroyer. Demara found himself behind the most seriously wounded Korean. Something, either a large caliber bullet or piece of shrapnel had passed through the front of the soldier's chest and gone clean through it and out, taking with it fragments of internal organ and bone. The smell of the wound alone was enough to nauseate him and he felt himself losing confidence once more.

"Come on, come on," he prodded the soldier. It looked cruel but he felt he had to get away from that soldier or come apart right then. When he reached the deck there were some nineteen soldiers stretched out along it, most of them smiling.

It is often the case with military wounds, since they are incurred in the field and are not immediately cleaned or treated, that they look far more severe than they are.

"There's less here than meets the eye," Demara said to Petty Officer Robert Hotchin, who was Cyr's medical as-

sistant. Hotchin had started down the line of wounded to
assay the extent of damage. At each soldier he began to slice
away the uniform wherever there was a wound but was met
by horrified cries of "Stop" and "No, no."

"Better not to treat the wound than cut the uniform," the
liaison officer said. "They will freeze to death in the winter."

No matter how painful, the Koreans preferred to have
Hotchin wrestle with their clothes and remove them. Demara's idea was to take care of the lightly wounded first since
they would have the most chance of surviving. The serious
cases, those who were close to death or whose wounds if
not treated would prove mortal he would treat last. It
seemed logical but the real reason behind it was delay. Deep
in the dark unknown of his mind he hoped the serious cases
calling for major surgery would die before he ever reached
them. Overhead there was another hope. A strong wind
had blown up and the sky had become overcast and then
dark with roiling storm clouds. They were in for a real Korean buster. He couldn't operate then.

Three of the nineteen soldiers were seriously hurt. All of
them, unless they received competent surgery within the
next day, would certainly die.

Demara cleaned and sutured and worked over the six-
teen, and as he did some of his confidence came back. He
could make incisions, he could clamp off bleeding, he could
handle sutures. What did he fear?

He knew perfectly well what he feared. The internal structure of the human body which he had never seen before. The
internal life of man where one clumsy mistake, one shred of
ignorance could cause him to take the life of a man and, for
all purposes, become a murderer.

For several hours he worked in the small ship's sick bay,
caught up in what he was doing, happy to find himself handling himself swiftly and professionally in front of the eyes of
crew members. But never before had he felt, at the same in-

stance, such an impostor and such a complete, lonely, isolated fraud. There was no place to run and no place to dodge what he had to do and no assurance that he could find inside of himself the courage or whatever ingredient it would take to begin surgery on the three Koreans who lay on bunks drugged by heavy doses of morphine.

"She's taking it well, Joe," Father Ward, the Catholic chaplain who also could assist at an operation, said.

"Taking what well?" he asked.

"The *Cayuga*. Taking the storm well," Ward said. "Those boys are lucky," he said, pointing at the three. "I think you're going to be able to work on them."

Work on them! The words sounded needlessly cruel to Demara and he wondered how Ward could say them.

"This is a lot of ship, Doc. She's rough as hell but she's steady rough. You can *count* on her roughness."

There was about the *Cayuga* a tidy toughness that sailors come to admire. She didn't go down into a trough and wallow in it and then get slopped all over with brine, coming up slowly and painfully one time and rising out suddenly another. The *Cayuga* went in quick and came out quick and set her own rhythm. She was the four things a great ship must be: resilient, resourceful, reliable and resolute. In her harsh way she was beautiful, like a brilliant mistress. She didn't love the men and she gave them a hard ride and yet despite themselves they had to love and admire her because she was all they had and the best they could find.

"Oh, I can't operate in this," Demara said. "Oh, no! Not one chance in hell, Father. Not one!"

"Then they'll die," Father Ward said. "Better to try than to just let them lie there and rot away."

"Father, I think this is my province," Demara said harshly. "Better to let them die peaceably in their sleep than to have them cut to pieces and murdered by a knife."

Ward looked at him. "I don't think so and I don't think

you do. I don't know what's behind your thinking, Doctor, and it's up to you. If you need help you'll know where to get me."

When Ward left, Demara turned to the seamen and officers still around. "Do I tell him how to save his bloody souls? Why does he tell me how to save mine?"

No one answered him. They all seemed to be looking away and through him. He went up on the deck and they were in a storm, a real storm. The wind was possibly reaching gale proportions. The only salvation was that it was steady, and the waves, small hills by now and topped with spewing foam, had a predictable pattern to them. The worst of it was that the *Cayuga* was riding it out beautifully. He felt a sudden burning desire for one long, deep draught of straight rum.

He went back inside the ship and down to the mess, where he opened the rum locker. He dealt himself four ounces of raw Barbados rum and let it burn the way down into his stomach. He didn't know why it helped. He wasn't drunk or even relaxed, but the drinking was something akin to a ritual that gave him some new reason for daring to begin again.

"Commander Plomer," he said, "I'm going to risk it. The sick bay is too small for major surgery. I'm going to have to commandeer your cabin. Have four seamen get everything out that can be gotten out, have them scrub the place from top to bottom and then have them go over everything with rubbing alcohol or disinfectant. I'll be preparing the patients."

And the blind shall lead the blind, he thought. Oh God, please help me now. I don't want to kill anyone.

Father Ward and Hotchin would help but that was scant solace. Not one of them had ever even assisted at an operation before. He went back down into sick bay and began preparing for the surgery. Just as long as he kept active the fluttery feeling in his stomach, which showed in his hands and in the twitching of a muscle over his right eye, did not bother him. Hotchin undressed, shaved and washed down each of the Koreans and kept them well doped with morphine. Demara sterilized his instruments, almost all of which he had never had a chance to use. Some of them he could never recall holding in his hand. He balanced the scalpel in his hand. That was the instrument he was afraid of. With that he would open a man and, in all likelihood, he would kill a man.

"We're ready now, Doctor," a young seaman whispered over his shoulder and the shock of it nearly made him cry out.

"We'll take the worst one now," Demara said. He really didn't want to know which one it was. Let the choice of the victim be up to fate or chance or ignorance.

"This is the worst one," Hotchin said. "Whatever hit him didn't come out. It's in there and it's causing him trouble. He's hemorrhaging."

How did the boy know that? Demara wondered. The thought that he did made Demara feel suddenly much relieved.

"Well, send him up," he said in a hollow voice.

The cabin was clean, and a bank of emergency lights, harsh and glaring, had been set up. The captain's long table, complete with straps for just such an emergency, was ready. Sheets were spread and his tray of instruments arranged and then the Korean was wheeled in by two seamen who looked strangely out of place. The lighting gave the scene an archaic, almost evil look, as if this were some ancient torture room, not a place of healing. It reminded him of a poster that used to be in the window of a drug store in Lawrence, in which a group of doctors, all dressed in full clothes, stared at the waxy figure of a man who was being operated on. It had always scared him and made him feel strange.

On the table, under the eerie lights, the body of the little

Korean had that same waxy look of death, only he hadn't died.

They really are yellow, he recalls thinking and he said it.

"How do you like that?" he said to Ward. "They really are yellow."

Ward merely stared at him in an uncomprehending way and Demara looked back down at the soldier's body.

The soldier lay on his back, trusting, defenseless, his arms limp along his sides, a jagged hole in his chest near the heart, but otherwise the skin smooth and unblemished.

That he was to take that knife and stick it into the exposed, bare chest of that man and then begin to pull it along through the flesh—the thought of that was too much to bear.

And he couldn't right then. He put down his scalpel and turned on his heel and went out of the room. There was no time for explanations or deception. He had to do what he was going to do. With no apology he went to the mess and once more opened the rum locker and from the heavy, copper-plated rum barrel poured himself a triple dram of rum which seemed to quell the fluttering of his heart and soul.

"Do you want us to head into the swells or take them on our sides?" Plomer asked. "Do you want us to go up and down or roll side to side?"

"I don't know," Demara answered. "Whichever is the most regular."

"Up and down," Commander Plomer said. "Joe, I just want you to know this one thing: you're in charge of the ship now!"

As he injected the tube which would carry the anesthetic, in this case an infusion of sodium pentathol, into the vein of the Korean, the soldier stirred and mumbled something which was heard by the Korean liaison officer.

"What did he say?" Demara asked.

"Well, he's only a peasant boy you know."

"What is it?" he demanded.

"He said," the interpreter said shyly, " 'May God guide your hand.' "

"You can tell him that I just made the same prayer."

The sodium pentathol was not strong enough to keep the soldier from experiencing pain and Demara was forced to use the old "open drop" ether system where ether is simply poured onto a cone that is fitted over the patient's face. He was afraid that the fumes might affect him. At last the patient lay completely immobile. There was an absolute silence in the room, broken only by the sound of gusts of wind at the porthole and the wash of seas.

"If You pull me through this, I vow that I will never deceive You again," he prayed, and then he lowered his cold scalpel onto the cold skin of the soldier, and began drawing the blade across his chest. It was amazingly easy. As the sharp blade passed along under the hole in the man's chest a thin red line followed along behind it like the wake in the path of a ship.

He made a straight, horizontal line, following the course of the ribs. Where had he learned to do that? he thought.

It was strange and marvelous and exhilarating. The knife moved easily, sure in his hand. It was as if he were now playing out some part which had already been predetermined. He knew exactly what he was doing and what he was going to do.

He was through the skin and now he found it even easier to cut through the layer of fat beneath that and then into the fascia, the white, bloodless connective tissue which holds the muscles together. He knew the words and he knew the right things to do. As he cut into the muscle he had to exert more pressure on the blade—the soldier was young and tough and wiry but he knew he was giving it just enough pressure to send the edge cleanly and steadily into the muscle.

"We've hit the bleeders," he mumbled to Ward. "He's going to bleed now. I'll need a sponge." With a surgical sponge he saw the first blood vessel he would have to tie off.

"I'll need a hemostat now. That. Clamp. That clamp there. Yes. That one, the clamp." He clamped the vessel and then tied it off, clumsily and slowly but neatly, with catgut.

In front of them, shielding whatever was in the soldier from their view, was one edge of the rib cage. The end is actually not bone but cartilage and known as the costal cartilages.

"Now, I'm going to have to saw part of this away," he said gaily, and several seamen who were in the cabin for emergency use left. He had not even a slight idea whether the sawing would be simple or hard or even if he could do it without piercing an artery or rupturing some vital organ.

The saw went back and forth like cutting through good dry soft pine. His fear was of losing the piece of cartilage down inside the man, something like dropping a coin through a grating, but it didn't drop into the body's cavity.

"Rib spreaders," he said.

"Rib spreaders?" Ward said. He wasn't sure it wasn't a joke, some kind of rookie's joke in which he is told to get some elbow grease or a sky hook.

"Oh, good Lord, Father. What can you do with amateurs?"

He had never seen rib spreaders used and had no idea how to use them but when he found them among the surgical equipment he knew at once how to handle them. He had a sudden and very distinct impression that he had done all of this many times before as someone else. He was a doctor reincarnated. He exerted traction on the ribs and they spread and beneath them they could see the pericardial sac and the heart which was pounding furiously.

"Look at it," Demara said. The idea that he had exposed a living, beating heart and the man still lived thrilled him. "Look at it beat." The massive muscle, the pulsating blood pump rose and fell. "It makes one believe again in God," he said.

The pericardial sac is a fibrous casing in which the heart and the roots of the great blood vessels are contained. The end of it near him was unnaturally red and raw and sore-looking, and somewhere in it Demara knew he would find the foreign substance lodged, a quarter of an inch from the heart.

"God help me. Blood," he suddenly called out. They had been neglecting to give the man blood and he had been bleeding badly. Hotchin set up a plasma transfusion.

Demara probed the pericardium and then he felt the object. It was metal and by the shape of it, it was the lead nose of a bullet. At that moment his objectivity seemed to leave him.

He had been lucky and he had been a fake. He now realized suddenly that he didn't have one single idea, or intuition even, whether to leave the bullet where it was and rely upon nature to eventually heal the wound or to extract it and in all probability cause a hemorrhage that must kill the man. He had had no real fears because he knew that this man would die, but now he knew that he might live and that it was up to him.

The area near the bullet was still bleeding and that was bad. He took a syringe and put the needle in the blood and drew it out and when he had cleaned the area in this fashion he could see the metal.

He looked at the darkness of the metal and the blood that once more was beginning to flow around it and quite suddenly reached over for a forceps, luckily got a purchase on the metal, and yanked. It resisted at first but then quickly and easily slid out of the pericardium leaving for a brief moment a cavity and then more blood.

"Gelfoam," he cried. "Where in hell is the Gelfoam?"

"In your hand, in your hand, in your hand," Father Ward cried. Gelfoam is a coagulant, and he flooded the wound with it. Then they waited for the sign of blood.

"If you have ever prayed very hard for anything before,

Father, will you begin praying harder that this doesn't hemorrhage?"

"I've been praying, Doctor, like I've never prayed before. It's really been sort of a miracle, hasn't it?"

"You really don't know how much of a miracle it's been," Demara answered.

There was no blood.

The rest was easy. His main worry was not to leave a clamp or sponge inside the soldier, so filled with Gelfoam was the wound, but Hotchin had had someone counting the instruments and they tallied. The going out was long and tiring because he was slow and crude with the sutures and his hands, unaccustomed to the strain, were tired. But two hours after he had begun his first patient was taken away.

"Well, Father, nicely done," he said. "Next patient," and as he did that he immediately was drenched in a flood of his own sweat. Somewhere within him a suppressed dam of chemical reactions, held in check by the enormous tension he was under, was released. Seamen and officers looked at him with astonishment.

"Always this way after a brutal one," he said wearily. "Amazing phenomenon, isn't it?"

The next two patients were more rudimentary. One of the two had a bad shell-splinter wound in the area of the groin. The main problem there was to clean the wound, to cut away sections of flesh, tie off a suspicious vessel and then sew up the area into reasonable shape and bandage it properly so that when it healed no muscle deformity would develop causing the man to be a cripple. What he felt to be the worst among cases was actually the least bad. The wound was cleaner than it appeared. Although it needed treatment for infection, the wound, which had gone completely through the body, had torn no muscle or bone tissue. But any direction up or down by a matter of a hundredth of an inch and the tough little man would have been killed at once. As it was, his chief complaint was that he couldn't puff properly on a cigarette. When he drew in almost nothing happened. Demara says that he recognized this as a partial collapsing of the lung, possibly caused by a fragment of rib penetrating the lung wall. To alleviate that he took a long needle, and using only a local anesthetic so that he could tell by the patient's reaction what effect he was making, he succeeded quite easily in creating a total collapse of the left lung.

During all of this time he never once noticed how much time was elapsing and he never once noticed the pitch and toss of the *Cayuga*.

"Oh man, we died up there," a navigator told him, "trying to keep that boat on as even a keel as we could. Every time we took a swell wrong I thought I could hear a man dying down below."

They turned out the bank of emergency lights and he was dumfounded to see in every porthole the faces of crew members pressed against them. He was also amazed to see that it was light outside. He had gone through the night and it was early morning. He knew that it was obvious, but he could not resist making the Churchillian sign of victory and the men cheered their doctor with a wild, spontaneous cheer. They weren't sure what they had witnessed but they sensed they had seen something very special and something heroic.

As he went down the passageway he knew a muscular, clean tiredness he had never experienced before. In the mess he stopped long enough to shake a few hands and to drink deeply of the Navy rum. He was keeper and only he could do what he did—drink from the barrel outside of grog time—but no man resented him his ration.

He went to his room after that and he slept possibly a day or two days, he had no proper idea. When he got up he felt better than he had ever felt before in his life. The sun was out and the sea was clear and blue and fresh.

"Good morning, Doctor," the crew said as he passed and he felt he did indeed own the ship he was on.

He belonged.

When he reached the sick bay, however, he was puzzled.

"Where are my little Koreans? Where are my patients?"

"Oh, them," a sailor said. "Someone came and began hollering at them and they all got up and climbed back down into the junk last night. They went over to Chinnampo."

He looked out the porthole across to a small island on which stood a collection of bombed-out and broken mud huts. Something very precious had been taken away from him, he felt, that he never could get back.

19

What happened afterward is surrounded by controversy. There were not many witnesses of what took place and none of these was qualified to judge what they saw.

The *Cayuga* went back to Japan to be refitted, and while there Demara wrote a long letter to Catherine telling her of his actions and admitting to her that that was the first time he had ever done any surgery. She was, of course, thrilled at the letter. The word of his exploits did not stop there, however. The *Cayuga* was visited by a young, eager press information officer who was starved for good, colorful copy. He seized on Dr. Cyr's story and he gave it the full treatment, adding colorful background material about the fighting ROKs and the Royal Navy. Just before the *Cayuga* sailed back, Demara was shown the copy.

"This is good standard copy," he was told. "It'll be placed in service papers here and it will go back to your hometown papers."

Demara's alleged hometown was Grand Falls but he made arrangements to have it shown instead in Halifax. In this way Catherine would be sure to see it, and he would be reasonably safe from Grand Falls. It was a silly thing to do but he was reacting to things with an easy largesse of manner. Halifax seemed so far away and the pressure from his fellow officers to release the story was strong enough to warrant his approval.

Two weeks after the operations the *Cayuga* was once

again in Korean waters and once more in the vicinity of Chinnampo. From the sick-bay porthole he could see the battered cluster of beaten-down mud huts that made up civilization there. Demara begged permission to borrow the *Cayuga's* launch and take it to Chinnampo to see if any of the soldiers he had operated on still lived.

It was early October when he landed at a rickety dock on the island and through an interpreter, he found his way to a long, low, windowless mud hut. Lying in the hut, in filth that equaled that in the junk, waiting for the comfort of death to close down around them, were several dozen Koreans. One of them was his first patient, the soldier who had had the bullet dislodged from the region around his heart. He was sick, undernourished, pale, and the dressing on his chest was close to rotting, but he was alive. The sight of it made Demara cry.

It is this that is controversial. The Korean interpreter, a Captain Hun Kim, went with Demara several times. Others from the *Cayuga* accompanied him from time to time and Father Ward went several times. Acting as if he possessed superior military rank, Demara says he took over control of the small island. Cleaner homes were commandeered for the wounded while the death hut was cleaned and scrubbed, supplied with a stove and given a row of eight windows. The whole building was then whitewashed and turned into an emergency operating room and field hospital. Every afternoon that it was possible to do so, Demara took the launch and operated. At times, when the *Cayuga* was close and contact was possible, he stayed for several days at a time, operating, treating civilians in the town, carrying out a sanitation program and, finally, treating the wounded from the battle lines who were carried by relatives and friends down to the doctor from the little neighboring towns to which they had been returned. It is here, following the step-by-step description of the operation in the British medical magazine *Lancet,* that he claims to have carried out a lung

resection—one of the most difficult of all surgical operations. His description of how he handled the problems involved was sufficiently convincing to persuade experienced
medical men that he might have done it, and he might possibly have succeeded, granting everything went in his favor.

"I don't think there is any reason to play humble about
it," he says today. "I was considered to be some kind of good
white God. I was loved and admired and adored. When I
went through village streets, crowds of sick and diseased
trailed after me like they must have once trailed after Christ
for a touch of the hem of His cloak. Frankly, considering that
half of them were doomed to die if they didn't get help, I
think I had more than my share of Lazaruses."

For the press information officer who was following up
on the Navy's "miracle doctor" this made an even better
story than before. Not only was the miracle surgery aspect
still alive but the human interest of Demara's selfless mis-
sionary medical work among our Korean allies added a
strong new dimension to the man. A second, much more detailed press release was prepared about Dr. Cyr and in the
middle of October it was shown to him for his approval.

There had been no repercussions from the first dispatch
and Demara had even less to fear this time. Also, his right
of approval did not cover stoppage of the issuing of the release, although that might have been done if he fought
against it hard enough, but only checking the facts. What
Demara did not know then was that this article, cleared
through Naval Headquarters in Japan, was then released for
all-Canada, general release. They thought it was a fine one
for the Royal Canadian Navy. The releasing of the piece
for general distribution was tantamount to what is known
as being "signaled" or "mentioned in dispatches" which is
tantamount in turn to receiving a high and much cherished
decoration for superior achievement. Another thing Demara
didn't know was that this kind of release was followed by
a trailer giving a full factual background of the man being

signaled. Everything the Navy knew about Dr. Cyr was compressed in three tight, factual paragraphs.

On the 23rd of October, according to notes belonging to Demara, he had an especially good day. He had gone ashore again and had performed an emergency amputation on a young Korean who otherwise would have died from gangrene within the week. The boy had not come to him; Demara had seen him lying in a woodshed ashamed of the stench of his limb. He also had come across the third of his first memorable three patients. The man was found among the women at the far end of a village near Chinnampo helping them flail grain and separate the seed from the chaff. In Korea this is women's work and he was ashamed to be found doing it but it was all he could do at the time. Almost anywhere else in the world it is considered hard, demanding duty. Demara examined the wound and while he found it ugly and raw it appeared to be in passable condition.

"The ability of this incredibly hardy Korean peasant stock to endure and survive goes beyond medical explanation. Someone (me?) should do a paper on this subject," he wrote.

"He says," Kim said, as they were leaving the soldier, "he is sorry to ask you but do you have one cigarette to give him?"

"Good Lord," Demara said. "I did a better job than I thought. This is the one whose lung I collapsed."

"He says, lung all better now. He doesn't cough any more."

That was the cause of great mirth. "Then I really saved his life. He probably was dying of tuberculosis and I saved him."

That gave him an especially rich feeling of accomplishment and that someone very good was, at last in his life, working on his side.

On exactly that same day and, very possibly, at the same hour, some ten thousand miles away from the drab shame of Korea, in the town of Edmundston, a few miles north of

Grand Falls, Dr. Joseph Cyr was getting tired of answering phone calls, asking if he had been in Korea or was it his son or who was it. He had not seen the newspaper accounts but he listened to one over the telephone from a Toronto newspaper and then from the Edmundston paper.

"There are lots of Cyrs in the world," he insisted. "Lots of Joseph Cyrs and even Joseph C. Cyrs."

For a few hours that reasoning was convincing, but then it was reported that that might be so but that he was the only Dr. Joseph C. Cyr in Canada. He was then read the credential section of the official signal. And finally a picture came down from Ottawa. This time there was no more reason to doubt. Dr. Cyr was deeply shocked.

"Why, this is my friend, Brother John Payne of the Brothers of Christian Instruction."

That was really sensational news. "Hold on, now," Cyr warned. "It isn't that good. He's really a doctor. This is Dr. Cecil B. Hamann. He was only a novice with the brothers."

Without consulting the Navy, first the Edmundston and then Toronto papers broke the news. When the Navy, in Ottawa, investigated they were quickly convinced that they had had an impostor foisted on them. In their words "a message was dispatched to the Commanding Officer of HMCS *Cayuga* instructing that the medical officer be suspended from duty immediately, that he be taxed with imposture, and a report to be forwarded to Naval Headquarters forthwith."

That was the official position, but man rarely acts quite as the dispatches trust he will.

20

He was lying on his bunk, reading, he insists, Lloyd Douglas' *Doctor Hudson's Secret Journal,* when an officer tapped on his door.

"Joe, the old man wants to see you."

Good, thought Demara, and I want to see him. He had learned by this time that he had been signaled, but the import of it had missed him. He hoped it meant he would receive some kind of decoration which he could then send along to Catherine but, even more important, would represent the first official award of merit he had actually won by his own efforts. No matter what might happen, this he could always be proud of.

When he entered the captain's cabin, Commander Plomer was visibly upset. "I have something here that I am not even going to comment on. I happen to feel that there must be some terrible or foolish mistake here but I don't want to go into that. Joe, I have got to charge you with being an impostor and to suspend you from duty."

The reaction of Demara was exactly what Plomer had assumed it would be.

"He was flabbergasted," Plomer reported. It was as if he had actually pierced the man with some kind of weapon.

"But this is crazy. This is madness," Fred cried out. "This is some crazy mistake. This is some insane plot. Don't move. Now, don't move until I come back," he shouted.

Once outside he didn't want to stop. He had to convince Plomer that a mistake had been made. He sensed deep within

him that it was all hopeless and helpless but he had a deep
need to, at least right then, if only for one more day, convince Commander Plomer and the men on the *Cayuga* he
was all that they wanted him to be.

He came back to the captain's office with an armful of
documents.

"There," he slammed down his birth certificate. "And
there. And there."

There is no question that Plomer was convinced that some
tragic or else hilarious mistake had been made. The documents were all passed on by the Navy and genuine. The man
had done his duties, as he said "with such zeal and energy"
and he apparently had done them brilliantly. And, not the
least of things, "he was greatly liked and respected by the
ship's company" which in a tight ship means a great deal. He
was, next to Plomer, the most popular man aboard.

"You go back to your room," he told Dr. Cyr, "and we'll
try and get this mess straightened out."

He went back to his room and in great self-indignation
picked up his book again and began to read. There are times
when men are capable of great self-delusion, which can be
a blessing or a way to ruin.

"Ridiculous," he remembers muttering. "Just *ridiculous*.
The whole thing simply an outrage. The nerve of Plomer
even to bring it *up*. That took some gall right there."

And then, with the suddenness of an explosive fire in his
room, the truth crashed down on his head.

"Catherine," he shouted. "Catherine, what have I done to
you, what have I done to your beautiful life?"

He began to cry and after that he became hysterical. How
long this lasted he doesn't know but he recalls running down
through the ship, crying out, "Captain, Captain, help me,
help me."

In Plomer's quarters he lost complete control of himself.
He demanded to be returned to CANAVHED (Canadian
Naval Headquarters) that minute. "Get me a helicopter. I

deserve one," he cried out. "I have got to have a chance to clear my name. My name must be clear of every mark on it at once."

He had to be forcibly led back to his cabin. He was not placed under guard. There was no chance this time for the tactic of French leave, once so reliable. But neither was there a desire for it. For the first time he was not alone and un-committed. He was taking another person down with him. That night he managed to get through the ship and into the mess and to the rum. How much he drank and how much he secreted on his person for future emergencies he doesn't know. The next day he was summoned to the captain's rooms but he was incapable of acting coherently. At first Plomer thought he was the victim of a mental breakdown, which was partly the case, but the next day they realized that Dr. Cyr was quite possibly close to death from alcohol poisoning. He was, on October 26, transferred to the cruiser *Ceylon,* in a state of paralysis, by a cargo sling.

"Tell them I'll be back," he is alleged to have mumbled in a heroic gesture. It was the very last thing he said aboard his beloved *Cayuga.* Once on board the *Ceylon* he woke long enough to notice the black boots and leggings of a man by his bunk, and look up quizzically.

"That's right," a friendly voice said. "The Royal Marines. You're under arrest, Doctor."

The next thing he remembers, before flying home, was peering out along the waterfront of Kobe and seeing a large sign painted along the docks—Yankee Go Home.

"That's not for us," the Marine said.

"The hell you say," Demara said. There was life in the corpse at last.

Under escort of a medical officer and a security officer he was flown back to Canada to be turned over to Navy Head-quarters in Esquimalt, B. C. During the flight he was grilled heavily by the security officer and he feels that he handled this phase of the affair well. As in so many cases with Demara, the organization involved stands to suffer from publicity of his case as much as he does. In truth, everyone involved except the public would just as soon forget it if there is a legitimate way to do it.

He admitted having entered the Navy fraudulently, he admitted that he was a practicing surgeon named Cecil B. Hamann, he intimated he had had personal problems in the States that forced him to disguise himself and flee, and, finally, he actually produced a doctor's certificate made out in his name with the seal of the State of Maine stamped on it. It was notarized by a large legal type seal, such as notaries use, with the name of Hamann embossed on it.

The one thing the Navy did not want to hear or learn was that Cyr was actually not a doctor. As a doctor he could merely be discharged and sent out of the country and justice could be said to have been done.

At Esquimalt he was placed under house arrest or, gentleman's arrest. He was free to move about on his word as an officer, a thing which still impresses him. Outside of planning his defense his main worry was whether Catherine had as yet discovered the real Dr. Cyr. He knew of no way to tell her.

During the course of their investigation, the Navy discovered that Dr. Hamann was actually Dr. French and Fred W. Demara. While in the Navy as Cyr, however, under his own initiative he managed to get a license to practice medicine in England and all the countries on the British Commonwealth, plus having a license pending in the United States. Legally, as far as the Navy was concerned, Demara could now practice medicine. The people now interested should be the civil authorities, their adjutant reasoned.

On the 12th of November, Demara appeared in full dress before a Board of Inquiry in Esquimalt. In the words of the Navy, "This inquiry was exceedingly short."

It is possibly the shortest trial in history.

"Do you wish to make a statement about the allegation that you are not the man that you represented yourself to be?"

"Yes. I did enter the RCN under false pretenses under a false name."

"What are your medical qualifications?"

"I'd rather let that go if I may, please. I am perfectly willing to be turned over to the civilian authorities for whatever action they may wish to take. I have hurt the Navy enough. I might add that I am a doctor."

"This being true, you are summarily discharged from the Navy."

He was returned to confinement before undergoing the painful ritual of being drummed out of His Majesty's Service.

In the course of that wait, with the suspense and excitement of the trial gone, he was suffused with a deep sense of shame for what he had done. Only then did he realize that his mates on board ship and the parents of those men would in all likelihood want to try him for murder. To them, what he had done must have been a profoundly disturbing if not actually horrible thing. He longed to tell them that they were safe and in good hands and he didn't know how and in his confusion he wrote a letter he wishes he hadn't to the then Medical Director General of the RCN.

"Just a note to ask your forgiveness for the embarrassment that I know I must have caused you personally. Please do not believe the newspapers or the results of the inquiry. I know that may seem to be asking a great deal but please believe that they are only about 40 percent correct . . . I am a doctor, having received my doctorate in medicine abroad with the greatest honors . . . Please believe that the boys on the *Cayuga* had full protection every moment that I was with them . . .

With every good and kind wish, I am
Sincerely yours,
(sgd) J. C. Cyr

(Pick a name—I've probably used it)

His hope was that the letter would be published and relieve his sense of brooding families all over Canada hating the thought of his existence. It was never published.

On the morning of November 20, he received in his room a very large package which had been directed to him in the Far East but which, through some unusually alert mail clerk, was redirected to Esquimalt. He was that much of a celebrity.

He ripped it open, dreading what he would see, and in it, potted live in a wooden bucket, was a small, hardy Christmas tree. Under the tree was a Canadian ham and with it was a note.

I mailed this very early because I know the RN and wanted you to get this before Christmas. I'm sorry it isn't dandelions. Don't be a beast, my jo, and keep it all for yourself. My slogan is: Put a piece of Canada in their mess this Christmas.

Oh, how I miss you. Wherever you are, Joe, I feel I'm with you. Wherever you go, I go, and wherever you do go I want to go.

With all my love, for all time,

Catherine

In the afternoon mail another letter arrived. This one had been sent directly. It was also from Catherine.

Oh yes, you know how terribly hurt I was when I first found out about you, dear Joe. I would not be true to you to deny that at first I just wanted to die and wished that I never had met you. But then something strange happened to me. I woke up this morning, my jo, and knew that nothing had changed. No matter what your name is, I am in love with *you*.

Don't you see how simple it is? How simple and funny it is? I love you, not a name.

Please, will you come to me? All the things I have ever said are as true and right as when I first said them. I love you.

It's so simple like that that I laugh aloud when I say it. Can you hear me?

I have always loved you from that very first hour. I always will love you. Please come to me when you can. Or, let me come to you.

I don't forgive you because you have nothing to be forgiven for.

At the bottom she added, as a postscript, one more thought.

Isn't it strange? It's just like the start. I don't know what to call you by—and I love you. I did then. I can and do now. Good night, my jo, and come.

It was the deepest hurt of all. He went out of his room and to the commanding officer of his barrack at Esquimalt, where he demanded to be released at once under threat of embarrassing the Canadian Navy to an extent they had yet to dream of. He could not stay there and keep what was left of his sanity for another day. Whether his threat had any effect or not isn't known, but on the next day he was told to be ready to leave at once. That afternoon this notice was released.

Ferdinand Waldo Demara, alias Cyr, will be discharged from the naval service at Esquimalt late today, November 21, 1951.

This is the shortest and simplest statement that has ever been released to the press from Royal Canadian Naval Headquarters.

21

DEMARA IN THE DUMPS

After that came the time of the drinking and the time of the deep doldrums.

He had collected overseas pay and back wages for several months, and when he left Canada he had over one thousand dollars in his possession. The immigration authorities held him for several hours but although his record was black and unsavory they were amazed to find they had no charge to pin on him. Demara's one positive act was to plant the small pine on Route 99 outside of Blaine, Washington.

"If everything goes bad someday I'm going to go back out there—I know exactly where that tree stands—and hang myself from it," he has said.

After that, he was drunk. Whenever the pain of reality and the memory of Catherine thrust itself on him, he pushed it out again by numbing his ability to remember or think. He was drunk in Seattle and Salt Lake and in Chicago. He doesn't know how he got back to Lawrence but when he did he was broke. He had no more yearning to drink and he felt not that a new life lay ahead but that an old one was dead with nothing to take its place.

He was amazed to find that the magazines and newspapers had been badgering his family for weeks. Several of them offered a considerable amount of money if he would tell his story.

"You know something," he said to his father. "It just occurred to me that I never in my life have done a thing for either of you. That's how incredibly selfish I am."

Without telling his family he contacted *Life* magazine and gave their writer a long interview. For this he received $2500, two thousand of which he gave to his father and mother as a present. Then he decided to undergo the worst punishment of all; he decided to go straight, wearing the sackcloth and ashes of being plain Fred Demara.

He got a job as a guard-instructor with the Youth Authority in Massachusetts at their Institute for Child Guidance.

"This was going to be my penance for Catherine. If I had ruined one life I thought I might be able to salvage a few others and try to balance the thing."

He had not counted on the fame the *Life* article was to bring him. He was called in one afternoon after he had been there long enough to know that here he could do a useful job.

"Demara? Demara?" the superintendent said. "Isn't your real first name Ferdinand?"

Fred had already begun to take off the coat to his uniform.

"Aren't you the man who . . . ?"

He was out of the door and away. The pattern was to repeat itself with increasing regularity. Sometimes he was the cause of his troubles and sometimes they happened. In Kansas City, where he was working in a child welfare bureau, he was arrested and taken out of town by some keen-eyed cop who remembered his picture from *Life* and reasoned that if he was in town he was up to no good. The same thing happened to him in Pittsburg. After that, however, he worked for a year at the Wassaic State School in New York for mentally retarded children and he did so well that he received a promotion to Matteawan State Hospital, a hospital prison for the criminal insane. It was hard, dangerous, challenging work.

"But I liked it. Every day. I knew I was learning a great deal, a great deal that most men never even see. And I was mastering it. I could talk to those people and they could talk to me."

A thing that frightened him, however, was a growing feeling that he could no longer tell any difference between the citizens he met in Beacon, New York, outside the hospital and the inmates.

"It bothered me all the time. I seemed to have this hypersensitive attraction to the wildly insane. The worst offenders would sense it at once and walk right up to me. I began to think that I was crazy, too. I had good reason to think that, of course," he adds drily.

He began drinking heavily and soon he resigned. There were other places after that but today they are all merged in a sort of dull glow with small spots of brightness when he was sober and great stretches of darkness. He was just rambling, running from everything, trying hard to forget everything that had happened, and as is axiomatic when you are rambling—you sooner or later hit Texas. And somewhere along the way, he still refuses to say how, possibly for fear that a robbery charge might result, he came into control of the credentials of one Ben W. Jones, a Mississippi-born, Georgia-educated, proper Southern gentleman. The time of penance was passing.

22

He woke one morning in Houston and realized that he could not go on the way that he had been. He could no longer, merely by wishing to, seem to control his drinking which was getting to be something more than a memory deadener. He joined the Houston chapter of Alcoholics Anonymous.

With the generosity of AA, and the natural generosity of Texans, he was welcomed and accepted. To his new friends he was plain Ben Jones, better-educated than most, a superior accountant who was trying to live down a past life of drinking and shame. Through the help of AA he kept himself sober for several weeks and made a solid, good impression on people. Through one of the members he got an introduction to the late Bishop Clinton Quin of Houston, then the Episcopal bishop of Texas. Bishop Quin was a man who liked to help alcoholics get back on their feet. He was impressed with Jones as a man and with Jones's credentials. Jones, as far as the bishop could ascertain, was a graduate of Georgia State Teachers, had taken graduate training in Nashville and had taken courses in Texas until drink had gotten to him. Bishop Quin decided to risk it and on his responsibility recommended Demara to Mr. Tom Schumate, part owner and manager of the Lamar, Houston's big, fashionable downtown hotel. Schumate was equally impressed.

"I'm going to put you in the auditor's department as a starter and let you get the feel of things by working on the books. Now, do you think you can handle it?"

"That's what I'm trained to do, sir," Demara said.

It was probably the worst lie of his life.

"You can fake being a priest or a general and anyone pressed at it, for a few weeks anyway, could probably do a reasonable job running General Motors. But these books. There is nothing to fool, nothing to fake. You simply have to do it right."

His greatest fear was that if he made some honest mistakes and they were found by an auditor, and then he was found to be something less of an accountant and person than B. W. Jones, that they would suspect that the only reason he was there was to rob the Lamar blind.

He had the excuse that he was a bit shaky and at least had the help of the previous bookkeeper to break him in but that was not enough to cover for his complete ignorance of the subject. With some of his last dollars he bought every book and manual on "bookkeeping made easy" and studied them late into the night. To outgoing Texans he was a strange breed of man.

Schumate was convinced that all Demara needed was a little contact with the public to get over his recluse attitude.

"Big jolly fellow like you, Jones. No place for you back here with the books. I'm going to put you out front where you can make friends for us. More money, of course."

In truth, Demara hated it back there with the books. But he could not afford the chance of being put on public display for eight hours a day.

"I want to thank you, Mr. Schumate, but I just don't think I'm strong enough to resist temptation."

"Hogwash," Schumate assured Fred. "You can't lick it if you don't face it, son. You just get ready to move on out front."

"Yes, sir," Demara said meekly. He got ready to move out period.

While thumbing through the Houston *Chronicle* that night he happened upon the news that there were openings for lowly positions in the Department of Correction, a euphemism for the Texas Prison System.

The idea appalled and yet appealed to him. Where else could an impostor be that safe? The only people who would see him would, if any recognized him, be in no position to do anything about it. He also felt reasonably sure that people with his credentials did not too often apply for prison posts.

That night he did a clever thing. Instead of applying directly to the prison system he applied to the wrong place for a reason. He wrote to the head of what amounted to the Texas Health, Education and Welfare Department, saying that Bishop Quin and other prominent people suggested he do it, and introduced himself and his credentials. He was intensely interested in penology, felt he had a great future in it and was curious how he might get into that work.

A few days later he got a letter back from the director explaining that while this was not in his department's province he had forwarded Mr. Jones's letter to the head of the Texas Prison System, a Mr. O. B. Ellis, and suggested he arrange an interview.

Demara's plot was well launched. He had relied on the tendency of one big shot to always deal with his counterpart.

Two things had been accomplished. No matter how innocuous the covering letter to Mr. Ellis it always acts as some form of introduction or implies some interest on the part of the sender. It also got his letter in the hands of those up top instead of going through channels.

"Always go to the top where they can make decisions and where they are accustomed to make decisions. They not only work fast but they don't have second thoughts about how someone up there might like it. They're far more liberal and understanding up top in any organization. They hire the underlings to protect themselves."

A few days later Mr. B. W. Jones got a letter from Mr.

O. B. Ellis inviting him to come to Huntsville, home of the largest prison in the South, for an interview. If the interview were successful there would then be a check on his three previous employers and he would be required to produce eight character references from people who had known him over the past decade.

The first posed no great problem since he could control that. The second might prove a little more difficult if some of the people he asked to vouch for his character were to talk too freely.

The first thing he did was to mail a letter to Dr. Cecil B. Hamann at his old Commonwealth Avenue address in Massachusetts, requesting on the envelope that if he weren't there the letter be forwarded at once to Cecil B. Hamann, care of P. O. Box 1387, Houston, a post-office box Demara took out in his own name. When the letter did come back he knew that the building at least was still standing and he at once sent off another letter to the building superintendent explaining that due to a mix-up in records several documents meant for Hamann would be forthcoming at the Commonwealth address and would they please send those along to the Houston P. O. box. To facilitate this he enclosed two stamped envelopes with his address written on them—in pencil. Demara immediately sent off one bogus letter to Dr. Hamann in Massachusetts and several days later it came winging back in one of his envelopes so he not only knew his system was working, but he had a good stamped envelope from Massachusetts. He rubbed out the penciled return address and typed in—Mr. O. B. Ellis, General Manager, Texas Prison System, Huntsville, Texas.

Now things were covered, and Demara sent in the names of "previous employees" to Mr. Ellis. The fairly extensive Texas prison system questionnaire was sent out to Dr. Cecil B. Hamann, Director, Massachusetts Youth Authority at the Commonwealth Avenue address. It soon wound up in Demara's post-office box.

A second one was sent to Mr. Fred W. Demara, Manager, Institute for Child Guidance, Bridgewater, Mass. Since Demara had actually worked there this letter was forwarded to his home address in Lawrence where his mother, in complete innocence, then forwarded the letter to her son's address in Houston so the second questionnaire was tidily in hand.

The third went to Mr. Schumate at the Lamar which Demara felt he could leave alone. They knew only good about him there.

Demara opened the questionnaires and began to answer them himself. He was modest but not sparing in his praise of Jones and he especially played up Jones' ability to handle tough disciplinary cases, which actually was true.

To lend an official tone to the documents he had both of them notarized. Dr. Hamann's was notarized nicely enough with his own seal which, unless you looked closely, you would not notice was authorized for the State of Maine. Mr. Demara's was also notarized but the embossed seal was scrawled on in such a way that it was very hard to make out that this was also notarized by Dr. Hamann. Mr. Demara's letter was sent on Institute for Child Guidance stationery which Fred just happened to still have in his bag. He was thus continuing to live up to a fundamental rule: Never be at a loss for a letterhead.

The list of references was somewhat harder since he didn't legitimately know anyone in the past decade who could vouch for him and still be considered to be in his right mind. He seized the bull by the horns and threw himself on the mercy of his new Texas friends. He put it flatly.

He needed references and he had none. All he had been for the past eight years had been a drunken bum and a souse. Would they be able to tell a white lie and cover for a reformed buddy and give him a fresh start in life?

It was hard to refuse since each man would have to live with the knowledge that his refusal to help might be the refusal that would send this man back on the road to self-destruction.

He got four people to make positive recommendations and he got four more people to, quite unknowingly, make favorable replies. That is, he answered for them. He gave their names and they were queried by mail. The thing the prison people did not check was that the addresses he gave them with the four names were those of a gas station, a rooming house where Demara was staying, the Houston chapter of AA and an open mail box of a Rice Institute professor where Demara could quite easily collect any mail. He did not feel he was toying with a federal offense since, in purest theory, those letters were never really meant for the people whose names happened to be on the envelopes but were meant by original intent for Fred W. Demara, a piece of legal logic it is doubtful would stand up in court. One of the names he chose was that of one Tommy Barefoot because it amused him and because it somehow had a real authentic Texas twang. No faker would ever use the credentials of a Tommy Barefoot.

The documents from Massachusetts were handled in accordance with Demara's understanding of institutions. He took them by bus up to Huntsville, which is some 70 miles north of Houston and 30 miles north of Cut 'N Shoot, Texas, out in what they call The Big Thicket, a rolling, sandy, red-clay piney-woods country that breeds mean, stringy cattle, men and razorback hogs.

At the prison he simply dropped the already canceled letters on the reception desk and said—"These are for the manager." He knew exactly what would happen. The guard at the desk, not knowing exactly what to do with them, having no book or procedure on the matter, went and put them with the incoming mail so they could be distributed in a proper way.

A few days after that he had his interview. They were as delighted with B. W. Jones as he was with them. The job was not much as a starter, not much for a man of his background, but it was a beginning. If he wanted it he could begin at Huntsville as lieutenant of the guard.

"When?" he asked.

"Why, today if you want," someone told him.

"Good. You see, I'm all packed. It may sound egotistical, but I figured I was going to like it here and you were going to like me."

23

Huntsville was a pleasant surprise. The prison is large, highly organized and impeccably clean. The red-brick walls of the prison are covered with ivy and parts of the prison look more like an Ivy League college than do many American colleges. Huntsville is also the biggest prison in the South and is the Alcatraz—the maximum-security lockup—of the tough Texas system. To Demara, whose sole image of a southern prison was a remnant of seeing "I Was a Fugitive from a Chain Gang," it was all very agreeable.

His bosses, instead of being fast men with a bull whip and bloodhound, looked like clean-cut, thoughtful business-men. His immediate superiors were O. B. Ellis, R. C. Jones (no relation), E. L. King and T. T. Easley. He became, need it be stated, B.W.

For breaking in, Lieutenant Jones was assigned to guard duty out at Wynn Farm, a vast, sprawling prison farm several miles beyond Huntsville. That was a blow but he determined to make the best of it. He knew he was on trial.

There is about Wynn Farm a certain medieval quality. The outlying fields stretch away from the great hulking bastion of the prison, and in the evening the mobs of peasantry troop in from the fields to the confines of the walls. The guards "ride shotgun" on horseback, and in the evening they take on the appearance of knights surrounded by the rabble of serfdom. They are treated much the same way as knights of long ago must have been treated.

Beneath the outward appearance of a tight, well-run organization, however, as Demara was to find, were some major drawbacks. The Texas prison system is peculiarly fitting for, and typical of, Texas.

They have hired an efficient, forward-looking prison management and the penal laws remain hopelessly archaic and backward. The best management can do is to continually make the best of a basically bad situation.

The Texas attitude is simple. Prisons are for bad people. They are punitive institutions, not corrective ones. While you are in there you are being punished, not pampered. If while in there someone happens to see the light and get corrected that is so much money in the bank. But the guiding principle is to isolate man from society as a gesture of society's revenge. The belief is that he then won't do such a bad thing again. The fact that this is not even remotely supported by facts has never apparently caused the Texas legislature many moments of real concern. The theory is an eye for an eye with the state getting the hog's share of it. The prison system is, amazingly enough, self-supporting, quite possibly the only self-supporting prison system in the world.

There is one other legal drawback in Texas which was to have much to do with Demara's success there. Texas does not yet have proper laws governing criminal insanity. If you go mad in a genteel way they send you to a state hospital, but if you take out your paranoiac delusions by shooting down or cutting up people you are most likely sent to jail. The result of this policy is that there are at any given time several hundred complete, partial or potential mad killers in the system, threatening at any time to disrupt things in a manner that is at times hard to believe. These paranoids are not screened out beforehand but generally go through the usual routine until they do something serious such as beat, stab or in any way attempt to harm or kill either guards or fellow prisoners. Sooner or later they wind up in the maximum-security section of the Huntsville prison.

If a man acts bad in maximum security, and a good many will, he will get considerably less understanding than a bad-tempered ape would get in a zoo, for example. And if he continues to act bad he will finally be subdued by brute force or gas. Management isn't fond of this but they have no other facilities. The best they can hope in maximum is that a prisoner can serve his time in there without being killed by his brothers.

Bedlam was this charitable.

One last challenge is the nature of the Texas prison guard himself. Wages are low and many of the old guards, from previous regimes, hang on since new blood can't be found. Many of these are locally known as the "hard-ass" breed, "stand-up" boys who "cover the ground they stand on." Violence and force is their court of last resort and they are as inflexible and easy to move as the prison walls. Out on Wynn Farm, Warden B. B. Tubbyfill (as he shall be known) was just such a man.

24

"Ahm tellin' yew, son, hyere's what you got to know," Warden Tubbyfill was telling him. "Yew got yew some mean sonsabitches on this cheer farm and they gonna' stomp on yew ever chance they get. Yew know what yew goin' to do?"

He let fly a stream of tobacco juice that could have drowned a tarantula.

"Yew ain't never goin' to give them the chance."

That was the theory in its simplest terms.

Early in the morning the prisoners are lined up in squads, or strings, and then run out to the fields on the double by a mounted guard riding shotgun. He is a private but the men learn to call him cap'n. In keeping with the medieval aspect, there is an ancient ritual and method for all relationships.

"Ol' cap'n," a prisoner will cry. "I got to take me a crap."

Ol' cap'n looks around slow and careful until he spots a likely-looking spot. "You run your ass down to that bush, boy, and you see you keep that bush flaggin'."

If the bush were to cease to move while the man was behind it, indicating he might be running, the captain would have the right to unload his shotgun on the bush. On both sides, even if a man were hurt, this would be considered "fair and square"—the final, acid test of all prison morality and ethics.

This kind of behavior and ritual, which Demara never mastered, governed life at every hour of the day.

Another thing he never mastered was the art of "knowing

his niggers." "Knowing your niggers" means demanding a form of behavior from them which you mean so deeply that when it isn't observed you are truly and deeply driven into a murderous, insulted rage. Negroes in the South tend to recognize this breed and have found a million ways to get around it. They were never sure how to get around Demara.

There was, when he was first there, an epidemic of prisoners slashing the tendons—called the ham strings—in the back of their heels to keep from having to go into the fields and slave.

The Ellis plan was to simply leave them where they lay until the men came in begging for food and water.

Ol' Cap'n Tubbyfill, as representative of the "hard ass" sentiment, felt this to be an intolerable loss of face.

"Please, warden, oh, please," he begged. "Just give me a big ol' length of trace chain an' I'll go down an' beat those people in. I'll lace it to them, warden, or I'll die in the tryin'."

And he meant it and everyone knew he did. Many prisoners preferred this to all the rest.

"You know what I like?" he said one night, after a few fingers of whiskey. "I like the excitement of a real good break. Late at night, the lights flarin' all around and the siren goin'. Yew know, I haven't plunked me a good, lively boy off that fence in years now. I don't know what's comin' on with the youth these days."

Into this did the erstwhile monk and contemplative move. In theory he should have done badly but his knowledge of organizations helped him ride out the rough early days.

"Do you mind if I present a request to the manager, Warden Tubbyfill?" he once asked at an opportune time.

"Go ahead, son, I don't give a goddamn what you present to who," he answered, as Demara figured he would.

Within a week he was transferred from active guard to recreation officer in charge of setting up a recreation program.

"You goin' to wash their faces with powder puffs in the mornin' before you're through here, ain't you?" Tubbyfill growled good-naturedly. He didn't mind just so his own bailiwick wasn't encroached upon.

Expand into the vacuum!

Captain Ben Jones organized letter-writing sessions for illiterates. He set up checker and domino tournaments and the winner's prize was a half day off from the fields. He tried unsuccessfully to set up a study period and finally he asked for, and got, a pingpong table. A request was in for movies. To Tubbyfill this was arrant nonsense. To the watching Ellis, it was heartening.

There was, one noon, as was inevitable, serious trouble. A wild inmate picked up his tray and began pounding on the head of the man next to him. The other prisoners jumped out of the way because this meant sudden, violent reaction such as clubs, gas and, if it went on long enough, buckshot. This time, however, none of the three happened. Lieutenant Jones came through the circle of men quietly but with the soft voice of a kind father. He held his arms out to show that he wasn't armed.

"I don't want you to put that tray down, son, if you don't want to put it down. I just want to know one thing. What's troubling you and who's bothering you, that's all? Now you can come and tell me."

The two stood looking at each other, the one wild and untrusting and the other calm and immense and immobile. For what seemed a very long time they stared and then the inmate dropped his tray on the ground and Demara put his arm around his shoulder and led him from the room.

"Why, that ol' Cap'n Jones, he might just have got hisself kilt," a prisoner said admiringly.

"You want to see you a brave man, by God, that man's Cap'n Jones."

So he was a hero!

"It was strange. It was like Matteawan. I never carried a

gun with the insane because I never felt I needed it. I always do outside. I'm afraid of rational people. I figured that boy, like most of them, was afraid. He struck out like that out of fear."

He also was wise enough to avoid the classic cause of violence almost everywhere, the show of force with no out to save face.

"Put down that tray, boy," the course of action goes.

"Don't call me 'boy.' "

"Put down that tray or I'm goin' to begin beatin' on your head with this here pistol."

"Well then you better start beatin', *boy*, because I ain't puttin' down this tray."

Sooner or later someone always got hurt.

"Always leave them an out with honor and they'll almost always take it," Demara has discovered.

It did not take long for news of Demara's exploit to reach Ellis's office and he was called in. Although it was plainly noted on Jones' record that he was not in favor of capital punishment and that he would not use arms in the event of trouble Ellis dared the question.

"How would you like to come to the main prison and work in maximum security?" Ellis asked. "It's the toughest of the tough."

Demara said that he would like to see it first and was given a tour.

"There were people in there with eyes so wild and strange that it made me wonder if people don't really get star crossed or aren't reincarnated from lynxes and wolves and those moon howlers."

The guard who was leading the way kept filling his ear with warnings.

"Don't get too near them bars or one of those boys will brang you to them," meaning a prisoner, if he could possibly grab him, would pull him to the bars and begin belting his head against them.

"You see, sir," the guard explained, "we got here what you got to call psychotics. Yes, that's it. Psychotics."

"What're they?" Fred asked.

"A psychotic," the guard explained, "is a mean, hard-assed sumnabitch. Those boys are *bad*, Cap'n, real bad."

Such was the extent of psychotherapy at Huntsville's maximum security.

"To an ex-professor of psychology it was, you might say, a challenge not to be denied," Demara says.

25

There is no zoo in the United States in which animals are as
desperately caged as are the men in Huntsville's maximum
security. The cells are low, narrow and short and never can
a man extend himself. This alone is maddening enough, as
maddening as the company he must keep.

Never does a prisoner come in any form of contact with a
guard. The keepers of the den pack tear-gas billies, heavy
truncheons which can eject a tear-gas pill on need, vomit
gas, pistols, blackjacks, manacles, rifles and shot guns.

And the prisoners are equally armed no matter what the
authorities do. They can't have spoons because spoons are
turned into double-edged knives. They made the mistake
of allowing the men plastic toothbrushes and these became
murderous knives.

The worst punishment, far worse than a beating, is the
"pisser." This is solitary confinement. The name "pisser"
stems from the fact that the sole apparatus in the cells is a
small round hole, which is the end of a water pipe. It is
flushed several times a day. In between then the convict has
a choice of using it either as a latrine or as a drinking foun-
tain. The diet is bread and water. The prisoner is lowered
into the pisser and the longer a man endures it the greater
the hero he is. The longer a man does endure the more certain he is to be mad or to be becoming mad.

The pisser does strange things to men and everyone acts
in it a different way. Three hours is enough to break some

strong men and a month not enough to break another. It can make a kind of implacable enemy who will never rest until he feels he has gotten his revenge.

The warden who was running the maximum-security section made that plain.

"Now, I feel I have to warn you, Cap'n," he said. "These boys, they're thinkin' *all* the time, Cap. They're thinkin' all the time."

B. W. nodded sagely.

"But don't let *that* worry you," the warden assured him. "*We're* thinkin' too."

The place was run exactly like a den of lions held at bay by a breathless combination of force, fear and wit. Into it strode Daniel.

From the start he was possessed of a kind of monumental arrogance that was bred not from arrogance itself but from complete self-confidence. Demara had it firmly in mind that these people were for the most part sick children in need of a father and love and understanding.

"I found that almost all the time men will act about as good as you expect them to act. If you treat them like animals they'll act that way. Or like children. I saw that in the service. If you treat them with respect, then they try to act that way. I wanted to set up the idea that this prison was my house and they were my guests."

They watched him moving among the men, talking softly to them, leaning against the forbidden bars and making jokes, calling them "mister," using their formal names and asking their problems and they wondered how long it would be before he met reality. He was breaking all of the sacred rules of "fair and square."

"I don't know if I'd do it again. But I believed in it. I know this much," he says today. "I'd *only* do it if I believed it."

Prisoners have an uncanny aptitude for getting inside the cover of a man and reading him and they are especially quick to spot fear and weakness. They didn't know how to

take the new captain. He acted all wrong. He seemed soft
and yet they couldn't feel the nature of the softness.

Even the convicts said it. "Ol' Cap'n, he's goin' to get hisself kilt one day, you wait and see," but no one was doing it.
Very early the first incident happened.

"My, you really have troubles," he said to one glowering
young inmate.

"You are just so right, you fat-assed bastard," the man
said.

That was "pisser" talk. The guards and prisoners tensed.
Right now guards should open the cell door and prepare to
"brang the man out" by brute force.

Demara looked at him like a fond mother hen an errant
chick.

"My, my. *Mister* Thompson. The words you use," he said,
and burst into an outlandish roar of laughter. "I'm going to
write a letter home about you. You really have troubles."

No one knew how to take it.

There were more serious incidents, however. There was
the boy who had crossed a guard in some fashion and who
wouldn't come out of his cell. He stood in the rear of his cell
and held in front of him a little spoon knife. Demara could
see he was scared but that isn't always a solace. A scared
man can be unreliable.

"Open the door," Demara ordered.

"Don't come in here, Cap'n. I got nothin' on you but I'll
cut you." He looked almost sadly at Demara. "I got to cut
you," he explained. The ancient code must be honored.

"No you won't, son. Not if I don't have a weapon," he
spelled out. It was true that no one ever tried that approach.

The boy tossed that one in his mind, still holding the knife
ahead of him as if it were something alive that might jump
and bite him. Demara bulked through the door.

"Now, before we talk about this, hand me that knife," he
said.

"I can't *give* you the knife," the boy said. "That's too far."

"Then I'll take the knife away. That fair?"

"Yes, sir. That's fair."

Demara suddenly reached out and got the boy's wrist with his powerful grip. He pushed the boy back to the wall and squeezed and knocked the wrist against it until the knife clattered to the floor and he kicked it out into the hall.

"Now we can talk, right?"

"Yes, sir. Now we can talk," the boy said. He was far happier than Demara.

"I don't know if I could do that any more," he now wonders. "I never have figured what I might have done if I missed that wrist and he had started cutting me. I might have ruined the whole thing right then. Of course, that was B. W. Jones operating, not Demara. And old Jones," he muses, "he just couldn't do any wrong."

Old Jones, with Ellis's permission, began to establish new methods in maximum. Granted that the men were being punished, he argued, they had to have some way to work off their punishment and regain self-respect. He got movies for them and he began having schooling organized. He also established a schedule so that the men had a feeling that the day had a ritual and a movement to it.

"That they liked, but the ritual had to be rigidly adhered to. Any deviation from it had to be scrupulously noted and explained. That made it *their* day. My other rule was to be absolutely honest. Never minimize anything. Even exaggerate. The prisoners always expect the worst, anyway. This seemed to give them some self-respect."

B. W. Jones was establishing himself as one of the new liberal penologists who yet seemed to have his feet on the ground. It is one thing to hear about a person's exploits and another to see them. O. B. Ellis had that chance.

A young, erratic prisoner, threatened with a spell in the pisser, committed suicide rather than face it.

Demara had previously seen that the boy could not face life in the cages and had recommended that, far from re-

ceiving punishment, the boy's term be shortened and he be
hospitalized. He was borne out on that much. The boy cured
himself by hanging himself on a cell door.

A prison mob can react with the suddenness of a herd of
wild horses. An insignificant event can spook the group into
a stampede frame of mind when at other times a terrible
series of events will fail to trigger any tension. During an
inquiry into the boy's death, a prisoner in the cell above that
of the dead boy suddenly became hysterical, reacting vio-
lently and threatening to unleash an explosion that might
not stop until a major disaster had taken place.

"I don't know how he managed it. I don't know what he
did or what he said. But he knew how to handle that man
and the situation. I know I've never seen anything quite like
what Jones did on maximum security before or since," O. B.
Ellis has since said.

"Part of my secret has never been revealed. I was one of
the first to use tranquilizers. I read about them using them
at a hospital in Louisiana—still studying medicine just in
case, you know—and got the prison doctor to order some.
I also used phenobarbs. They're good, too. Once or twice
when no one was around I just knocked some real bad cus-
tomers down for a while with some sodium pentathol and
let them talk their frustrations away. You might say I was
Texas's hospital for the criminal insane. Think they'll ever
name one after their pioneer?"

After that, as everyone knew and will admit, B. W. Jones
was slated for rapid advance. His promotion to assistant
warden of maximum security—a rise of fantastic speed in
the organization where men wait thirty years to rise to captain, a feat Demara managed in a little more than a month—
was already assured.

"I can't deny it and I don't see why I should," O. B. Ellis
says. "B.W. or Demara or whatever it is you call him was
one of the best prospects ever to serve in this prison system.
His future was bright, if not almost unlimited. I can say this

—if he could only appear again with some legitimate credentials, and somehow this past was wiped out, I'd be proud to hire the man again."

Demara was quite conscious of this. His future was bright and unlimited, marred only by one thing; he still was deeply in love with Catherine.

"Oh, I wanted her to see me, doing what was right and on my own efforts. I wanted my family to see me, too, but mostly her. You know, there was a book I read by Albert Camus . . . *The Plague* it was, I think. In there a man is writing a book for thirty years and he never gets past polishing the first beautiful paragraph. That had to be just perfect. Once he got that down right, the rest would all come easy. I sat down night after night and started my famous letter to Catherine. Sometimes I wrote as many as twenty or thirty starts but I couldn't get it. Finally I didn't even know if I had the right to begin the letter dear or not and that would plague me for hours. Unless I was at the prison, which I was for as much as eighteen hours a day, I was completely miserable."

As Christmas of 1956 approached he increasingly had the feeling that something big was brewing for him. As a present he felt he was going to be made a warden. And always, in the back of his mind, was one of the six big prison farms spread out across Texas. That was too much to hope for then, but one can't control the fling of one's dreams.

At the same time the citizens of Huntsville were making a nice gesture. Boy scouts were scouring attics and basements of homes to find old books and magazines which would make good reading for the men.

"I thought it was a nice thing for them to do when I heard about it," Demara says. "Magazines aren't the best form of education but," he says ironically, "a man can learn a lot from them."

The magazines went through regular prison channels. They were searched to see if they contained any dangerous items in the pages and they were found to be harmless. On the fifth day before Christmas they went out to the men.

Oddly enough, Demara was not at Huntsville that day. He had taken his first day off to go up to Houston and air-mail some presents home to his family. And to Catherine. Even if he didn't send a letter he was determined to buy something entirely beautiful and send it anonymously.

26

There are many people who should not be in jail. They are too bright-eyed and too smart to be there. One month would do as much good as five years. The stigma is attached and the rest of the waiting is a waste of everyone's time. Such was the boy who, lying on his bunk after lunch, leafed through the magazine.

"I'll be a three-horned, mean-eyed, long-lifed bastard," he shouted. "Oh, this is great, man. Great."

"What is it?" his cellmate demanded, but he was too smart to say. "Guard," he cried out. "You better send that big captain down here. What's his name? Jones. Send him down right away."

The guard at first refused but there is a ring of authenticity about certain voices that compels attention. The guard knew that whatever was up Jones would be interested in hearing it.

Jones was not to be found. As the afternoon wore on the boy's secret grew too big for him. He showed it first to his cellmate who let out a whoop and a holler also. Finally he called the guard to the bars.

"I'm going to give you a peek at something," he said. He folded the magazine just so and brought it close to the bars.

"Why, that's Cap'n Jones," the guard said. "What's he doin' in that *Life* Magazine?"

"That's something I'm not telling," the young convict said. "But I'll tell you this. Mr. O. B. Ellis wants to see this thing right away. I think you better go get him and bring him right on down."

"Oh, hell," the guard said. "I'll just take the magazine to him."

"Like hell. You'd give it to Jones. I want to get something out of this."

"Then I'll come in there and take it," the guard threatened.

The young man ripped it from the magazine. "Before you open those gates I'll eat this thing."

Ellis was not at once available but that afternoon and evening a stream of lesser prison officials visited the boy's cell and were treated to some teasing, tempting, tantalizing looks at the famous issue of *Life*.

There was no question to any of them that the man billed in the article as The Great Impostor was their own Ben W. Jones. Later in the evening, in exchange for a choice block of seats at next year's famous Huntsville prison rodeo, the pages were produced.

A meeting was called at the home of Mr. Ellis and the top people in the prison attended it.

The first order of business was to agree that Jones did, indeed, seem to be Demara.

The second was what could they do to rectify it?

The third was what should be done to Jones?

None of these things interested O. B. Ellis. He was deeply hurt and shocked by what had happened.

"It was as if I'd caught my own son stealing," he said. "I was ashamed for him and myself and all of us."

The tougher types among the group had less emotional reactions. In the old Texas tradition there was some mumbling about horsewhips, tar and feathers and riding on rails, and then some cooler head, thinking of avoiding publicity, suggested getting the man lost in the bottoms of the Big Thicket where even cajun swamp rats feared to probe. There

are swamps in the Thicket where the earth has no bottom
and where if the quicksand and 'gators don't get you, the
water moccasin and cottonmouths will.

Mr. Ellis put an end to that. It was nearly eleven o'clock
at night and it had been reported to him that Mr. Jones
was home from Houston.

"You tell Mr. Jones, please, that he's wanted here right
now," Mr. Ellis said. He was not happy about facing the
man he had trusted.

He was stretched out on the couch of his little house out
near Wynn Farm. He had his own house with two houseboys
supplied by the prison. For the first time in his life he had a
sense of being a true man of property. When the knock came
at his door, he was watching television on a set he had only
that day bought and installed and the reception was even
worse than the programs.

"Cap'n," the guard said. "Mr. Ellis wants to see you
pronto. I think it's something mighty important, sir."

Demara could hardly restrain himself from leaping to his
feet and cheering.

"It's going to be a merry Christmas after all, Tiny Tim,"
he said. He went to get a tie and coat. "What's that, Cap'n?"
the guard asked.

"Nothing, my boy, but in the future call me 'Warden
Jones.'"

He was surprised to see the entire Ellis house lit up and
he was even more surprised to see, as he entered the large
main room of the spacious house, the room filled with quiet,
unfriendly, even surly faces. Only Ellis seemed to retain any
sense of graciousness. He rose and motioned him to a seat.

"Something serious has happened here today, Ben," he
said. "I think you'd better sit down."

"Oh, dear God," he murmured. "That's too bad. In maximum security, sir?"

"Yes. Maximum security. It concerns you as a matter of

fact." He held up the pages from *Life* magazine. "Is this you,
Ben? Are you Ferdinand Demara?" His voice had an indescribable hurt and sadness in it. To Demara's credit as an
accomplished impostor not one shadow or flicker of emotion
crossed his face. Within him he felt a sickening feeling of
despair and hurt. He wanted to cry out "yes" and end the
thing right there, but he knew he had to control himself.

"Why, no," he said, with an incredulous, quizzical look.
He did not look at the magazine right then. When he did
he allowed a look of utter disbelief cross his face.

"Fantastic," he whispered. "My God, this is me, staring
right back at me. Incredible. I've been told by people that I
looked just like some famous . . . What do they call them?
. . . Impostor. This is really something."

He looked up with a friendly, bewildered, disarming smile
on his face but the eyes that met his were cold and dead.

"This is you, isn't it?" Ellis asked.

"No, it isn't me," Demara said in a hurt voice edged with
anger. "Where did you get this? Five years, almost six years
old. Who dug this up anyway?"

"One of the men, a prisoner . . ."

"A prisoner. You heard it from a prisoner and you took his
word before even bothering to ask me about this? You took
his word first?"

"We didn't take any prisoner's word, Mr. Jones. He
merely . . ."

"He merely was reading the magazine and noted the re-
semblance and the guards and wardens came running,
didn't they? Now I'm ruined here. Did it ever occur to you
people that every convict in Huntsville will think you're
covering up for me . . . a crook?"

He felt he was turning the corner beautifully and swing-
ing the entire questioning onto another level. He remembers at the time actually feeling a thrill of excitement at the
masterful way he felt he was handling his problem. He had
thrown doubt on the recognition and he had most certainly

thrown serious doubt on the way it had been handled. If they were wrong, then they had acted badly.

"And another thing. I can get to believe in my causes. I was hurt that they suspected me, one of their own. Deeply hurt. For the time at least I think I forgot I was guilty. I became the wounded party and I think I played it to the hilt. Texans are very honor-bound and prideful and they knew they had impugned my honor. They don't like to do that. I just poured it on until I had real tears in my eyes and made plenty of them feel weak and humble for doubting me."

At the door he left them with his parting shots that apparently scored well.

"Yes, I am ashamed. I'm ashamed for myself and I'm ashamed for every American who was ever asked to admit his guilt before even being confronted with the evidence. This is a sad day for me, gentlemen. And I think it will prove a sadder one for you. I am going back to my house now and pray for the strength to endure this insult and see if I can find it in myself to try and forget and start again."

In the silence of the room he started out of the wide doors but he paused.

"If there is still any among you who feel I am guilty of this accusation I'd like to ask him to rise and face me now."

Many of those present looked to Ellis. It was apparent that most still felt he was guilty but were no longer entirely sure of the evidence at hand. Mr. Ellis made no sign.

"I will meet him at any time and in any fashion in which he chooses. My honor dictates that I can do no less. Everyone knows where I can be found."

At the door he slipped on his new five-gallon cattleman's hat he had also got that day in Houston. He hoped it gave him the hard, resolute look he admired in a man.

"Good night, Mr. Ellis. Good night, gentlemen, and may God help you."

It was a stunning, a smashing performance. It topped easily his plea before the Navy court-martial. The least he achieved was time. He had made his peers reluctant to prosecute him. When he went out the men crowded around the magazine again.

"It's him, all right. I mean it's just got to be him."

"And yet we've got to be sure. We could never forgive ourselves if we made an error. Never," O. B. Ellis said. The men agreed. "I think we had better start to work on this right now."

Back at Wynn Farm, Demara was already at work. Turning out all the lights in his house except one small, yellow bulb he began stripping his house of everything he valued and carrying it out to his new Chevrolet. He worked with a relentless fury and although the night was cold in only the way Texas can get cold, he was sweating right through his coat. In twenty minutes he had loaded his car in a wild, slapdash fashion and then he got behind the wheel of his car and waited.

"Maybe I am a much harder person than I know but all I kept thinking, sitting in the dark behind that wheel, waiting for the chance to slip and run, was—Why in God's name didn't that crook who found the thing try to bribe or blackmail me? If it was me then he knew he was dealing with a guy he could bribe. That's what I mean about Texas. Even the crooks don't know how to act right."

From the car he could see the lights of the prison and he suddenly felt a desire to give up and sleep. But the lights also returned him a message. They were burning late with an unusual intensity and it was all for him. The thought of becoming a prisoner at Huntsville sent a shot of adrenalin scurrying through his body. The lights of a large truck were coming up the highway and he could hear the roar of the Diesel motor from far off. When the sound got very near he started his own motor and by the light of its headlights he began down the long lane toward the main highway. He waited until his eyes grew accustomed to the night and then he slipped out onto the concrete and rolled down the road back to Huntsville and Houston beyond until he was far enough away from Wynn to flick on his lights.

It was one of the strange feelings of his life to glide through Huntsville's dark, quiet streets, wrapped in the anonymity of his car, driving through a place he had learned to love and where he had felt the worthwhileness of existence only to learn that it was eternally his fate to find a home and lose it.

"How many times I have died and how many times I've been orphaned," he has said.

27

DEMARA AND THE LAW

The weeks after remain only a blur to Demara. He drove to Houston and early that morning he cashed a large check at the Lamar Hotel. As he was leaving the lobby with one of the employees, the morning editions of the Houston papers were being untied and stacked. The headlines were hard to read at a distance but Demara's experienced eye had little difficulty recognizing half of the face of Ben W. Jones. He steered the man clear of the newsstand, and once safely on the street, he ran.

His one desire and ambition at the moment was to get out of Texas, not an easy thing to do. The main roads east would be staked out and the ones going west ran eight hundred miles, a haul that he couldn't afford. On the outskirts of Houston he managed to get his hands on a case of whiskey, and in the hamlet of Pointblank, he began drinking it in the hopes that the nirvana produced by alcohol might in some fashion award him an answer. He was consumed by the fear of being taken in Texas and serving time in the Huntsville prison. It would only be a matter of time, he felt, before either the caged or the cagers killed him. The happenings from Pointblank on are vague. He recalls a terrible time in Louisiana, where a minister was running a Christmas revival in a tent in which Demara was the number one item under discussion. He sat hopelessly drunk while the preacher alternately reviled him and prayed for him, and Demara would sporadically rise to his feet to announce what a terrible disgrace he was and that the Red River, on which the town was located, ran red from the broken heart of his mother.

After being washed in the waters of salvation but not purified by them, Demara somehow made it all the way to Key West, where he found he couldn't drive any farther and stopped. There he cashed a check in the name of B. W. Jones on his Huntsville Bank. The check was in Huntsville perhaps five minutes when an alarm was sent speeding from Texas and Demara was arrested. He simply didn't care any longer. Among the charges filed against him were embezzling (for cashing a bad check in Houston), forgery, stealing a car (the car he was driving was not paid for fully), imposturing, defrauding, resisting arrest, vagrancy, drunkenness and, in general, making a monumental public nuisance of himself. All told, the charges could bring him something like forty-seven years in jail, a thought that was sobering. He prepared to marshal a defense that would make his performance before the Navy pale by comparison.

The major tactic, his point of massive resistance, was to evade Texas by refusing to agree to extradition. To aid his efforts to avoid extradition he decided to hint that he knew of some deadly crimes in Florida that they would never find out about if he were in Texas. After gaining time in this way he would get out a series of letters to various Texas officials threatening to blow the lid off their departments if he ever was pulled into Texas again. The only charge he felt he couldn't handle was the one of drunkenness since he hadn't even been capable of staggering when apprehended, but this he was ready to face. Ten days in the lockup in place of forty-seven years in jail would have to be considered some sort of major triumph.

The actual proceedings were an anticlimax. Texas didn't want Demara. The last thing they wanted in the world was the sight of Demara's hulk looming across the state line bringing with him all the embarrassment he represented. They were not eager to put one of their public errors on the stand for the whole world to see. And O. B. Ellis was not a vindictive man.

"As far as we were concerned, outside of the original deception, Jones or Demara or whatever you call him," Ellis says, "had done nothing wrong. He'd been one of our most qualified men. I didn't want to hurt him. And I didn't want to see him."

The wire services got word that Demara was in jail, and his story was news again. Without his knowledge Demara's mother covered the bad checks. The car was returned and one by one the charges were dropped as the erstwhile Darrow stood, his mouth open, reduced to silence as the crimes melted away. During his stay in jail, the men of the *Cayuga* and some of his old messmates sent him a large Christmas card, a picture of the old ship, with Berton Braley's poem— "Loyalty"—written on the back. It goes this way:

> *He may be six kinds of a liar,*
> *He may be ten kinds of a fool,*
> *He may be a wicked high flyer,*
> *Beyond any reason or rule.*
>
> *There may be a shadow above him*
> *Of ruin and woes to impend,*
> *And I may not respect, but I love him,*
> *Because—well, because he's my friend.*

Of all his mementos he is most proud of this one. The students at North Haven later on printed the poem in full in their yearbook with no comment.

The State of Florida sprung Demara after several weeks suggesting at the same time that he remove himself from the scenes of his crimes. He went home to Lawrence.

Contrary to what he had always believed—that he would

get some mysterious premonition when there was serious trouble at home and he was needed—he received not even a faint suggestion that while he was in Texas his father had died. Demara had a feeling that a major phase of his life had closed, and also that with the fiasco out of Texas he had lost his last chance to accomplish anything big or meaningful or even really decent.

"Those were my days of remorse," he has said. "I didn't know any longer how to face my mother, much less myself. I'd walk down the street and see a leaf being picked up by the wind and sent scurrying down the street and I'd think of something. It would make me think of something."

He would remember that cold, wet day they followed the moving van from Jackson Street or think of the things he had never done with his father or the things he had done to him, all the words left unsaid and the things undone, and then he'd think of himself, as aimless and unable to direct and control the flow of his life as was the leaf its direction.

"I had sad eyes so large that I must have looked like those pictures of beasts in the slaughterhouse. I wanted someone to come along and slaughter me humanely."

One of his troubles, he feels, is that life in America, because of a loss in values, has become so soft and understanding that things no longer have meanings.

"I had no way *to* repent. Wherever I turned, people forgave me, because they were too understanding or, worse, they just didn't care. Here I was, a martyr to a compulsion that was killing me, and there was no executioner at hand."

He had to repent to himself, always the most difficult form of repentance. For a time he renounced drinking and the simple pleasures of life and cut himself off from life.

"I didn't realize it at the time but I was doing the Trappist bit again. I was purging myself and that was good. At least I got enough self-respect back that I could see a leaf again or not bust in tears at the sight of some sparrow out on the lawn looking for crumbs in the snow."

There was something imperfect about his repentance, however.

"I told myself and I promised myself that this was the end. I was going straight the hard and the simple way. But way in the back of my head I didn't believe myself. After all, I am a reasonably smart man. Would you if you were me?"

28

One day he felt his strength had sufficiently come back to him to allow him to face the world once more. He left a note on the kitchen table and he was gone.

Under his own name he got a job working in a children's home in western Massachusetts but that didn't last long. He was soon known and he left. In New York he then signed on as Frank Kingston in a school for mentally retarded children in Brooklyn.

"The name Kingston was not impostoring. Anyone could have had the job except, perhaps, Demara. I didn't want to embarrass myself or the school any more."

Although he liked what he was doing, his old enemy, boredom, reappeared. As a result of his most recent exploits, this came more quickly now. Any job that Demara can legitimately expect to hold is far beneath him. If he tries working in a hospital it isn't long before he finds himself peeking into the operating room, dreaming of the feel of a scalpel in his hand, knowing once more the overwhelming and urgent sensation of men's lives depending on your knowledge and skill, dreaming with a far-off look of the challenges that could await him. When the dream passes the sense of empty boredom in his real station becomes intolerable and the blood of the impostor begins to flow once more through his veins. It is never very long after such a dream that he goes.

"I tried hard as Frank Kingston but as Kingston, I was a bore and I was bored."

On the radio one afternoon Demara heard about the predicament of North Haven School, destined to be teacherless out in the cold and cheerless waters off Maine.

"It was exactly as if a trumpet call had sounded Charge. At the end of the program I turned off the set and started to work getting the right papers. I didn't wait a minute or think one minute about it. I was just doing it, as if it were a work preordained."

His acquisition of credentials was, however, not an act of fate. By judicious use of N. Y. State Board of Education stationery, which he stole, and Brooklyn College papers which he borrowed, Demara managed to acquire the completely adequate credentials of Martin Godgart.

His rise and fall on North Haven have already been chronicled. What is not known, but which certainly would have rated at least cursory notices in the various local papers is that Demara, after being uncovered on North Haven, went with this writer on a tour of most of the places where he had once impostored.

At Gethsemani, when we were asked had either of us ever been there before, Demara very coolly and believably answered, "No!" On a tour of that awesome and inspiring monastery, our guide at one point quietly turned and said, "Ah, and this is new since you've been here," and the hardened impostor blushed, if it is possible, to the very root of his soul.

At Gannon College, which now has approximately 1,500 students, 80 teachers and not-one-Dean-of-The-School-of-Philosophy, in a burst of exuberance, Demara scrawled such things as *F. W. Demara, Jr. was here* and *Join the Pious Order of St. Mark* and we talked to many professors about the old days, but apparently no one was aware of the intruder in their midst.

In Arkansas, to prove to me his versatility, Demara, in front of a hostile audience, made a speech for integration of the races.

"Man, can't he talk. I don't like *what* he says but I like

the way he says it," I was told. "That ol' boy ought to be a Baptist minister."

After the trip, having reviewed once again all the errors of his past, Demara tried for a time to go straight. He went to New York where he felt he could live in anonymity. But as Demara he could not get a decent job any place, and one day, with no word except that he was leaving for the tropics (and he exhibited two tropical suits to prove it), he left.

Months later there was a small notice in the Washington *Post* that a Martin Godgart was wanted by federal authorities for breaking a federal contract and for failure to pay an airplane fare from Point Barrow, Alaska, to Los Angeles. Subsequent investigation proved what anyone might expect, that the Godgart in question was the same Godgart as the one in North Haven who wasn't Godgart at all. Demara had used the same sullied documents to get a job teaching at a small Eskimo-Indian school on a trail outside of Point Barrow, which lies well north of the Arctic Circle and not too far south of the North Pole.

"It was thrilling to me," Demara has since communicated. "I had a feeling there of being able to somehow rejuvenate myself and, well, rearrange destiny. I think the relentless cold and enormous number of hours of quiet and darkness did that to me. And talk about a power vacuum. I could have preached a class in Communist doctrine and no one ever would have known."

And then along the trail came some old, long-memoried trapper who had years before read that article in *Life* and who never forgot a face.

"How that man could possibly be so egotistical or cocksure about his memory I can't understand. There we are, literally 3,400 miles from a hot bath, and he says, 'You're that famous faker, aren't you? What's it worth to you for me to keep my mouth shut?' God! I should be the greatest living advertisement and proof of the impact that *Life* has on the public memory."

He left on the next plane. One warm night a few weeks later in Los Angeles, Demara was watching "The Bridge on the River Kwai" and it occurred to him that he could make a bridge if he had to. The possibility excited him. The next day, under an unknown name, Demara applied for a job at the Hughes Machine Tool Company and obtained what could pass as some official credentials. After that he got the civilian credentials of two engineers, one named Carl Shelby and one named R. C. Spingarn.

The bridge project, of course, would have to be a simple one and he scoured lists of help-wanted ads until he found one that suited him perfectly—bridge builder wanted for work on rural roads in Yucatan, in southern Mexico. Rather than apply for the job in the United States, Demara went to Mexico on the basis of very sensible reasoning that his papers, which looked phony in the States, would pass inspection in Mexico, especially after he did a lot of highly professional doctoring on them.

He never had a chance to make a bridge and see if it held up at least as long as the one over the Kwai. Trouble developed in Yucatan over the time limit on his working permit, and Demara knew he could not stand any form of official scrutiny.

"They might have taken it hard to find that their skimpy funds were being manhandled by the likes of me. They might even have taken it worse that the bridge I would have built would probably have fallen down with some citizens of Yucatan on it. I had managed that long to avoid the Texas jails and I was damned if I was going to try a Mexican version."

From Mexico City, traveling this time as B. W. Jones, Demara went to Cuba. His intent, he says, was to run a good Cuban prison. He had read somewhere that prisons there were filled to overflowing and experienced prison authorities were desperately needed.

"I didn't care which side I ran the prisons for, I meant to

run a good one. If the place was full of Castro's men I intended to run it right, and if I had to work for the rebels, then I would run it right full of Batista's men, if any were left alive to put in jail."

There is some suspicion that Demara also had some faint romantic idea of running arms to Castro. One of the "important" prisoners in the Texas prison system was a hardened gunman who before his capture had made big money running arms to Castro's fighters in the Sierra Maestra Mountains.

"Oh, yes, ol' Cap'n Jones and The Fox (as the gunman is known) were close as thieves," I was told.

An apt phrase!

Whatever his plans Demara never had a chance to implement them. The Batista government, under tremendous pressure, naturally had a great interest in anyone coming in. The authorities sensed or knew something was not right, for Demara didn't stay long. He was impounded and then padlocked on the next plane back for Miami.

He went back to New York, and, unable to get a job, thinking only in terms of trying one last big caper and feeling unable to react any longer to reality, in a lucid moment, after a great deal of drinking, he turned himself in at Bellevue Hospital to see if the psychiatrists at that famed and experienced place could give him a clue to controlling himself.

He was a terrible patient. Ever since his days teaching psychology, Demara had little faith in psychiatrists. After the first hour, he was of no use to the doctors or himself. But it was for Demara a splendid experience which he is delighted to have suffered.

"I was exhilarated because I learned one thing. Those insane people in Bellevue were *really* insane. Even if I tried I couldn't act as nuts as those people. Oh, I'm a neurotic, a serious one but I'm controllable. When I convinced myself

I wasn't crazy, I got a whole new lease on life. It seemed to give me hope and meaning again."

The meaning in Demara's life has always been hard to isolate. But in his own strange way Fred Demara has actually made some distinct accomplishments in life, ones that to some very small degree have affected every one of us.

"I don't mean this to be boasting, but my lurid example—there's a word for it—has been instrumental in getting colleges and businesses to change their sloppy ways of handling confidential information and records. At several national conferences, because of me, codes have been drawn up tightening the whole procedure. In other words, your privacy and your records are safer today because of *me*. Isn't that grand? Isn't it uplifting? I've ruined myself for myself."

There is no question but that the security procedures of the Texas Department of Correction have been altered. If it is any solace to those with sons and daughters in Texas jails, their chances of having a crook as warden are much reduced.

"But then, you never can tell in Texas," Demara adds.

Demara is quite possibly the only Massachusetts northerner to serve in any modern southern prison. Outsiders are notoriously unwanted in southern penal systems.

Also he has very likely been in more Catholic orders and institutions than any Roman Catholic alive today and the list is not necessarily complete. As incredible as it sounds, Demara still feels himself to be a devout Catholic, although even he admits to being a misguided one. Somewhere in the back of his mind is a belief that God is going to find a way to help him cleanse the spots in his past and allow him to be reborn with all innocence into the Mother Church.

"The role of the Church is to hate the sin but to love the sinner. The duty of the Church is to extend its helping hand and grace to the reformed. I feel it only fair to say that I am serving notice that I am only waiting to feel a true call again before once again trying to find my meaning in the service of the Catholic Church."

However, because of his very activities, the Church in the United States has been prompted to reëxamine some of the aspects of its testimonial-letter system as a way to checking on the qualifications of its religious candidates.

"I know one step they could take right now but I'm not going to tell them, at least until I am on the inside looking out again."

He has been told that his idea is perfectly apparent and revolves around the Church's adopting the police practices of identifying pictures and, especially, fingerprints.

"Well, I hope they have the decency not to do *that* just because of one or two corrupt men. Think, a great devotion might die on the ink of a police blotter."

And at least partially because of Demara's prodding a college exists, LaMennais College in Alfred, Maine. Apart from Demara's influence, it has one other distinction. It is the smallest, four year, accredited college in the United States, boasting twenty-four pupils and five teachers.

"And to think, I had dreams of turning it into the Notre Dame of the North. I can say one thing about the place. It would be a bit difficult to field a football team and have a band all at the same time. Do you think if I came back wearing another's plumes, as we impostors like to say, that they might give me another chance?"

The answer is no.

29

THE REASON WHY

On January 25, 1959, newspapers all over the country once again blossomed with stories about Ferdinand W. Demara, Jr.

Genius Without Portfolio Unmasked Again, one headline read.

Gentle Masquerader At It Again.

The Great Impostor Wanted, others put the news.

It was a story like many others with perhaps significant differences. The school board of Winchendon, Massachusetts had just discovered that its fine teacher of English, French and Latin, Mr. Jefferson Baird Thorne, who had quit mysteriously in November, was in reality an impostor named Fred W. Demara. School Superintendent Meacham appeared to feel that Thorne was a "genius." He was not wanted for fraud, but for payment of $294 in back pay, an oversight Demara is rarely guilty of.

Allegedly, Jefferson Baird Thorne was a graduate of the College of William and Mary, but at that Virginia school they had no record of such a name. Demara's forgeries this time were not based on real credentials but were hasty, clumsy documents. He left mysteriously because, as an experienced hand, Demara senses the right time to leave. Mr. Thorne was due for a hasty de-thorning, and none knew it better than Demara.

And once again, from everyone who knows or reads about the man, comes the question of why. Why has he done it again? Why is his face once more staring out of the pages of newspapers? Why is he once again, lonely and rootless, restlessly on the run across America?

Psychologists and psychiatrists have made many guesses, and perhaps many of them are correct. There is no question that Fred Demara owns some of the classic background that might lead to impostoring. At an early age he lost his social status and all that went with it, and many feel that he has been going through life in another guise trying to find it again. Whatever the reason, here is a man who is driven by a compulsion so deeply rooted that probably only lengthy analysis could provide clues and motives to his conduct.

For all of the theories that have been advanced, however, perhaps one of the wisest was said by a man on North Haven.

"By God, you know, all of the time he was out here I always had the feeling that he was laughing at us. Not hard, you know, or nasty, but laughing like he was enjoying a great big secret all his own. Oh, don't tell *me*. He was having a real lot of fun posing."

No psychiatrist would be willing to buy that simple analysis, and yet the simplest truth about the man is that life suddenly and almost miraculously becomes exciting and challenging the moment he drops his own cloak and puts on the protective plumage of another.

It is a game and, at times, a great game. It is tense, it is serious and funny, it is dangerous. It is self-expanding at the same time that it is self-destructive.

It is also a heady opiate that, once tasted, makes everything else seem flat and stale and, even unreal. It is hard to avoid the idea that even as this is being read that urge to experience one more wholly satisfying draught of the drug—the one caper to end them all—hasn't once more seized his fancy and carried away his soul again.

Just a short time before this book was completed I received a phone call from an unidentified place.

"I'm on the biggest caper of them all. Oh, I wish I could tell you," Demara's voice said on the other end. "I'm sorry about that book now. Oh, I am sorry."

"So what are you doing?" I asked, which is an old dodge which never works with Demara.

"I can only tell you this. I am not you and I am not Huckleberry Muckleroy." Mr. H. Muckleroy is an old mutual Texas friend. "I wanted you to know, anyway, that I'm doing *good* things."

"Good for you or for humanity?"

"Why, shame on you. For both of us, of course. Apart from Catherine I've never been more happy or excited."

Even as he said that I sensed I had lost contact with him.

"Apart from Catherine . . ." I heard him repeat but in that strange, withdrawn, lost way he can assume. There was a very long pause since neither of us knew what to say.

"I'm working on that difficult part of the book we talked about. You know the part," I finally said and at once wished that I hadn't.

"What part?" he growled. He knew.

"Where you tell me why," I said.

In a voice as cold and as dark as the night air outside my window he said, "Because I am a rotten man."

There was another very long and embarrassed pause.

"I told you that the first time I saw you. I'm telling you now for the last."

I was going to hang up but he was talking again. The crisis and memory had passed and his voice was completely different.

"All right. Tell them this, and this is the truth. On Christmas Eve over San Diego, California, before a host of believers, I will be drawn to heaven by a fiery chariot. I will be umasked. The secret will be finally revealed. I am a Saint!"

I was silent.

"All right," he said. "Tell them this then. I have thought

it out and I believe it's truth. It's rascality, pure rascality!"

He hung up and I stood there thinking because it oc-curred to me that that is perhaps exactly what he is: the champion rascal of his age; one of the last sad playboys of the western world.

ABOUT THE AUTHOR

The son of a writer—Kyle Crichton—ROBERT CRICHTON was born thirty-four years ago in Albuquerque, New Mexico, when herds of wild horses still ran across the mesa that surrounds the city. The Crichton family moved to New York, living in Queens, Bronxville and on the East Side of Manhattan, and then moved to Newtown, Connecticut.

Robert Crichton attended Portsmouth Priory, a Benedictine school in Rhode Island, where, he says, he was a good athlete and middling scholar. From the priory, he entered the Infantry during World War II as a rifleman, where, in his words, "he fought and ran for the Republic" and eventually was bombed out of action in the Battle of the Bulge. On his discharge, under Civilian Capabilities it says in its entirety: "Person capable of firing and cleaning M-1 rifle."

According to Mr. Crichton, he left Harvard after four years of such courses as Celtic and Russian, still able to clean a rifle. He became a professional letter-writer, a chicken rancher (author's note: the big blow of 1950 ended that venture), and finally a free-lance writer.

His most famous article was published in the *Saturday Evening Post*. Entitled "We Must Shoot More Deer—Now," the article still draws a dozen letters each autumn from animal lovers, who invite him to the woods to be shot. He has rejected all offers.

Mr. Crichton is married to Judy Feiner. They have four children.